MEET THE PLAYERS IN PROJECTLAND

DECIDE THE RIGHT PROJECT ROLES & GET PEOPLE ON BOARD

A PROJECT GURU PLAYBOOK

DAWN MAHAN, PMP

PROJECT GURU PRESS

PRAISE FOR MEET THE PLAYERS IN PROJECTLAND

"The first, most important job that a manager has is fielding the right team. The intent of this book is to help project leaders do just that."

- WHITEY HERZOG, HALL OF FAME BASEBALL MANAGER

"Skip the snooze-fest! This book is your wild guide to project success, with fun animal metaphors and practical tips to build winning teams."

- CORNELIUS FICHTNER, PMP, AUTHOR, COURSE CREATOR, AND HOST OF THE PROJECT MANAGEMENT PODCAST™

"People are the fuel on which an organization runs, and leading people to deliver projects takes special savvy in this regard. This is especially challenging for the new project leader or anyone who struggles with the variety of personalities and agendas that commonly surface. This insightful book gives pragmatic guidance in a fun and colorful way with real-world examples and is a must-have resource for every professional's desk."

- JERRY MANAS, AUTHOR OF *NAPOLEON ON PROJECT MANAGEMENT*, *MANAGING THE GRAY AREAS* AND MORE

"Novice and experienced project people alike will learn how to successfully handle those 'gotcha goblins' as Dawn Mahan leads you on an educational, creative, and visionary journey through Projectland, so you can navigate the terrain like a pro."

- JESSE MIDDAUGH, PMP, MSIS, PENN STATE UNIVERSITY PROFESSOR, BASEBALL FACULTY MENTOR & ICE HOCKEY ADVISOR

"Though I write about workplace culture, and have had to spearhead major HR projects, I had no idea about project roles until reading Meet the Players in Projectland. Anyone can benefit from the insights in this book. There were times I laughed out loud, and the content kept me interested in learning more. The author's leadership style and personality shine throughout, making it a page turner."

"A fun, easy read laser-focused on the biggest driver of project success--the people. From your first project to the C-Suite, this book helps you create a team and culture designed to accelerate strategic IMPACT."

"Learning how to manage the people-part of projects takes years of experience and hard knocks, especially the ability to predict and interpret hidden agendas. Fortunately, the author's animal metaphors make it easy to quickly remember the lessons. This book is worth reading from cover to cover, as well as for reference. I am personally putting the lessons to work straight away."

"Whether you are new to project management or are an old salty project manager looking for a brush-up, read this book! Dawn takes a fun approach that's truly informative, using clever animal avatars as accurate stand-ins for the people you're likely to encounter in your project journey."

"I got more insight into my field of project management from this one book than I did from 25 years of experience. As I read the beginning of the book, unsurprisingly, we were revisiting familiar concepts. But then I realized I was understanding the concepts in a whole new way. It was as though I was carrying an expert project manager AND a coach in my pocket. And when I discovered the Valley of the Indecision Dweller, I knew this book was definitely for me."

- RUTH PEARCE, AWARD-WINNING COACH & AUTHOR OF *BE HOPEFUL, BE STRONG, BE BRAVE, BE CURIOUS* AND *BE A PROJECT MOTIVATOR*

"Great project managers are like those amazing team players who set the standard of excellence for everyone and help make all their teammates better. They become the heartbeat of your organization. Dawn's approach is living proof that those players aren't just born, they are made.

She's done that for me twice in very different settings to great success. Her practical approach doesn't just build project management capacity in your organization—it helps change your culture."

- RICH NEGRIN, ESQ., FORMER NFL PLAYER, FORMER PENNSYLVANIA SECRETARY OF ENVIRONMENTAL PROTECTION, AND C-SUITE EXECUTIVE

PRAISE FOR DAWN MAHAN'S EDUCATIONAL PROGRAMS

"A unique way of explaining project management that doesn't feel like I'm at the dentist!"

- RAOUL DAVIS, ASCENDANT GROUP CEO, AUTHOR, INTERNATIONAL SPEAKER

"I learned more from Dawn in one hour than I did in most of my college business courses."

- RYAN BIRCHMEIER, VP MEDIA RELATIONS – NEW YORK

"A brilliant course...totally affirmed my thoughts on the PM role itself and has re-energized me for my future career!"

- LARGE GLOBAL TECH PARTICIPANT – LONDON, ENGLAND

"This was an excellent course! Lively, interesting, and engaging presenter who kept my attention. I didn't want to miss anything."

- CAMPBELL'S PROJECT LEADERS – HEADQUARTERS, NEW JERSEY

"Excellent course. I am mentoring someone now as they consider a project management career path and will highly recommend this course."

- JUNE N, ABOUT *SMART TIPS: PROJECT MANAGEMENT & AGILE*

"Clear, concise, and funny!"

- RACHEL M, ABOUT *SMART TIPS: PROJECT MANAGEMENT & AGILE*

"I really enjoyed the last 8 weeks. I have a new understanding and appreciation for projects, how they work and what's needed to make them successful. But, I'm also thankful for the new confidence I feel in my work. I really needed this class!"

- GABRIELLA, GLOBAL MARKETING LEADER & PRACTICAL PROJECT MANAGEMENT (PPM) CERTIFICATE GRADUATE – PHILADELPHIA, PA

"Dawn's 'sponsor school' unlocked some critical insights that served as rocket fuel in our journey to greater organizational and strategic clarity, collaboration, and efficiency."

- TANYA CARLSON, DEPUTY CHIEF OF STRATEGY

"I was looking and I couldn't find anything quite like it. It was brilliant. Thank you!"

- ZEENA H., SENIOR MANAGER, MARKETING INTELLIGENCE & PRACTICAL PROJECT MANAGEMENT (PPM) CERTIFICATE GRADUATE – LONDON, UK

"Dawn's commitment to understanding our learning needs and desired outcomes was evident from the very start. What impressed me the most was Dawn's ability to stimulate interest and engagement among the executives."

- WILLETTA LOVE, ASSOCIATE DIRECTOR OF PROJECT MANAGEMENT & PROCESS OPTIMIZATION

"I've been attending meetings for 2 years and this was my favorite."

- PMI CHAPTER PARTICIPANT OF *DECODE PROJECT MANAGEMENT: GET YOUR GAME ON!* – PENNSYLVANIA

WHAT IS A PROJECT GURU PLAYBOOK?

Our Project Guru Playbooks are brief, action-oriented guides that are designed to be:

- Fun
- Focused
- Newbie-friendly
- Practical

With this playbook in hand, you should be able to implement its pro tips on your project immediately to increase your chances of success with less stress.

MEET THE PLAYERS IN PROJECTLAND

First Edition, April 2024

ISBN-13: 9798990411708
ISBN-10: 8990411708

Published by Project Guru Press I Summerland Key, FL

For the nervous, newbie project person, who deserves someone to introduce them to an easier path through Projectland.

PROJECTLAND

PROJECTLAND [NOUN PROJ-EKT-LAND]

1. A concept to convey that projects are like a different world with different roles and rules.
2. Consider Projectland a place with a capital P like Pluto, Poland, Pennsylvania, and Philadelphia. Each have their own terrain, challenges, and opportunities. When traveling to a new place for the first time, it's best to prepare.

ORIGIN

Dawn Mahan coined the term *projectland* first without the Capital P prior to 2018, when she blurted it out during a live, corporate training session. In 2020, passionate Book Insider VIPs insisted it be capitalized like a real place.

She applied for the trademark in 2022, and it was officially registered for training and workshops in 2024, so we began using the ® symbol. She subsequently applied for Projectland to be trademarked for e-books and printed books, as well. This is why we currently have the TM in certain places, pending offical approval. So if you were wondering why we appear to be having a trademark identity crisis, now you know, and it's because we are. In fact, it's driving Dawn nuts that it doesn't match everywhere.

Because it's really annoying to do so, we will not continue to show the trademark every time we mention Projectland in the book. The Projectland image above was developed in 2023 by Beth Montgomery in collaboration with Jerry Manas and Dawn Mahan. We all hope you like it, and that the concept helps you to embrace and conquer this wild world.

"There are some things you learn best in calm, and some in storm."

— Willa Cather, The Song of the Lark

CONTENTS

SECTION FOUR
BONUS CONTENT

INTRODUCTION: A NOT SO FUN FACT & WHY YOU NEED THIS BOOK

"Of all the things I've done, the most vital is coordinating the talents of those who work for us and pointing them towards a certain goal."
- Walt Disney

Did you know that MOST projects FAIL?

They cost too much, take too long, the thing doesn't quite work as expected, some important people got upset along the way, or the final result falls short of expectations (if it gets delivered at all). Often, several of these unfortunate circumstances happen, and then, the project that we thought in the beginning would be great, turns into a really dark cloud of dirt that hovers around us like Pigpen in Peanuts[1].

Even some of the biggest, best-known brands have experienced epic project failures. Software glitches have been blamed for releasing prisoners early. Construction projects notoriously take too long, cost too much, and are disruptive as all get out.

In the book that Inc.com called "The most important business book of the year[2]," *How Big Things Get Done*, by Bent Flyvbjerg and Dan Gardner, the authors shared these startling statistics after analyzing 16,000 projects:

- Only 48% achieve the cost goal
- Only 8.5% end on budget and on time

- Only 0.5% end on budget, on time, and deliver the promised benefits

But why and how does project failure happen?

Did you know that lack of proper management support is a top reason for project failure?

A survey of seventy professional engineers[3] suggests that there are at least a dozen distinct explanations for projects that flop with a capital F. The respondents were presented with seventy reasons for project failure, asked to rate each reason by its importance as a cause of failure, and to select the five most important reasons.

They found that the top three reasons for project failure were:

1. The project was not adequately defined at the beginning.
2. The project manager was incompetent.
3. There was a lack of clearly defined project goals and objectives.

These top three can be eliminated by leaders engaged to define the project clearly and assign the right project manager in the beginning of the project.

Additionally, "lack of support and involvement of top management" was specifically identified as another top reason for failure. Indeed, even if leaders do a good job addressing the top three reasons for failure at the start of the project, they can't then wave a magic wand and say, "make it so and let me know when it's done," and then exit stage left and disappear. They need to remain engaged throughout the entire project. Since support and involvement are two different things, let's unpack them a bit.

Upper-level management should continuously make it clear that the project is worthwhile and that they support it. They should also get involved at the appropriate times and in the right way. Hence the advice above about *proper* management support. The *proper* clarifier is not only because inadequate support is detrimental, but also because over-involvement by upper-level management can contribute to failure, too. Over-engagement of upper-level management often undermines the project manager's authority and the respect of team members, subcontractors, customers, and others.

In effect, attempts by upper-level management to over-control the project can result in a project that gets out of control. The role of upper-level management in a project is not to be the project manager, but to be a sponsor, facilitator, champion, and key decision-maker of the project. The duties of a sponsor will be explained in Chapter 5. For now, keep in mind that involvement by leadership needs to be "right-sized" for the project. Like the Goldilocks fairytale, we're looking for leaders to be involved not too much, not too little, but *just right*.

Change was cited as another major cause of failure, including situations where upper-level management had changed the scope of work.

Other survey suggestions from engineers regarding upper-level management's involvement in project management are that projects sometimes fail because of the "owner meddling in the project manager's affairs" and "team members being removed from the project for long periods of time to complete other company tasks." Borrowing project team members for other tasks after they have been assigned to a project can cause the project to stall out.

None of this should be a surprise.

Who gets projects done? People.

Who sabotages projects (on purpose or by accident)? People.

Who can help you succeed or fail? People.

Not Trello. Not Microsoft Project. Not any other tool or process.

Even the tech wizards at Microsoft reported that human leaders are critical to success, citing "weak executive support[4]" as a top reason for project failure. In the article, they stated, "Having an executive sponsor with a vested interest, someone who will go to bat for your project from start to finish, is a big factor in project success. Yet, fewer than two in three projects had actively engaged project sponsors to provide clear direction or help address problems. Lack of time is often an issue."

Successful projects happen when the right people are assigned to the right projects at the right time and are afforded the time and space to focus. One of the most important things to get right in the beginning of any project, is to identify and organize the RIGHT people into a team. This includes identifying the leadership team, as well as the superstar Subject Matter Experts (SMEs) for your project.

Just like every basketball player—from budding newbies to professionals—needs to dribble, pass, and shoot the ball with a reasonable level of skill, so, too, do you need to get foundational skills right to have any hope of succeeding and not feeling foolish in your organization. And just like every athlete practices to get good at the basics, so must you. Don't worry if it feels awkward at first. You're building skills and confidence with every shot you take at setting your project up for success.

For twenty-five'ish years, I've been living, breathing, sweating, and even dreaming and waking up in a panic about Projectland (a term I use to describe the world of projects—we'll explore this later in "Chapter 2: Welcome to Projectland"). Both as an employee and as an award-winning project management consultant, I've been fortunate to work across industries, inside giant global businesses with names you'd recognize, small businesses, and seemingly every size in between, because projects are happening everywhere. I've learned a lot from not only the miles I've personally logged in Projectland, but also from the thousands of learners in nearly 100 countries who found themselves seeking an easier path through Projectland's unexplored terrain and trusted me to be their tour guide. Their challenging questions have sharpened my own skills and helped me find simpler ways to explain how to navigate this wild world with ease in *most* situations.

I say *most* because each organization and each project situation is unique, and the beginning part, where we'll spend extra time in this book, can be especially so. This uniqueness is where the Projectland "gotcha goblins" lurk. Of course, every human in Projectland is unique too, and whether a project is seemingly simple or seriously complex, the fact is that it is the *people who will make or break your project*. Since most people haven't been prepared to navigate Projectland properly, *it's worth it to take the time to get the people part right*. Getting the people part right applies to you regardless of your role. From top leadership to summer interns and everyone in between, learning the roles and rules will position you to contribute positively. The uniqueness factor means we should not expect any one person to have all the answers, and that good ideas should be welcomed from everyone.

A case in point is one of my keen college students, Sebastian. I was hired to be the first project management instructor for the YearUp[5] program in Philadelphia at Peirce College. Students were largely from tough city neighborhoods who would not otherwise have access to good jobs at major companies. My role was to help prepare them for internships, so I based the "Practical Project Management for Young Professionals" course on what I teach inside corporations to professionals of all ages and experience levels. Plus, we added a micro-certification to make sure that students had the opportunity to learn the Project Management Institute (PMI) process in a fun way using my *ProjectFlo® Process Learning System.*

Sebastian was a model student, worked hard, and earned the micro-certification. I followed up with him for a one-on-one video call to see how he was doing in his internship at Merrill Lynch, a Bank of America company, and what I learned from him will always stick with me. He said that, while he works in operations, projects are constantly rolling through his department like a freight train disrupting things. His boss had recently held a meeting to talk about one of the next projects that was on its way. Sebastian said he visualized the process he'd learned through the micro-certification and asked a few probing questions based on what he'd learned in class. His boss's reply was that those were very good questions, and he didn't have the answers yet, but he promised to go get them! Indeed, the student intern who understands Projectland not only added value to his department that day, but also elevated his standing by asking just a few basic questions.

These are some of the results that I trust you, too, can experience when you understand how Projectland works. In addition to sharing my "best of" material from consulting, training, and coaching over the years, I will attempt to point you to the right rocks to look under in your version of Projectland, as well as the questions to ask so that you can find your way and help your team prepare to win.

While statistics show that most projects fail, yours doesn't have to. As the authors of *How Big Things Get Done* warn:

- You won't succeed without an "us."
- Know that your biggest risk is you.

They also advise to "be a team maker." By the end of this book, you'll be prepared to do just that. You'll be able to identify and avoid improper management support on your projects and set yourself and all of the people involved in your projects up for success!

To accomplish this, I've organized this book into three sections.

In *Section I: Welcome to the Jungle*, we'll cover critical foundational concepts including answering a question asked by a seasoned, savvy hospital administrator, "What is a project – really?" in Chapter 1. Once you're clear on what a project is and what it's not, you'll be ready to be warmly welcomed to Projectland in Chapter 2. Here you'll discover why this term and concept has helped our organizational clients and thousands of learners embrace the right mindset to succeed in a world where the odds are stacked against you. In Chapter 3, we'll address the common question, "Is project management just like management?" I'll also share the term I prefer to use instead of project management and you might too.

In "Section II: Meet the Players of Projectland" I'll introduce you to the typical who's who in Projectland with the help of carefully curated animal avatars. You will:

- Learn to speak the language of professional project managers related to roles and responsibilities on projects
- Meet our animal avatars that help explain the characteristics of common creatures in Projectland and make learning fun
- Be able to identify the key players on your projects, determine who's who, and assess where you fit today
- Be prepared to suggest special skills that might be helpful to have on your project team

We will dive deeper into each of the key players, starting at the top of the typical project organization, dedicating a chapter to each one, as follows:

- Chapter 5 – I'm the Sponsor, Hear Me Roar
- Chapter 6 – The Steering Team Is Not a Committee: Eagles, Whales, & Owls, Oh My!
- Chapter 7 – The Project Manager – Not Quite the King (or Queen!) of the Jungle, but Awfully Close
- Chapter 8 – The Dream Team – The Fast, the Strong, & the Furiously Fun
- Chapter 9 – Three Surprising Kinds of Stakeholders

At this point, you'll have a foundational understanding of Projectland and the creatures you may encounter during your journey. You'll figure out where you fit and know what to expect from everyone else.

In "Section III: Get 'Em On Board & Ready to Rumble," we'll cover practical tips to help you determine who you need to help your project succeed, how to get them on board, and ultimately how to get them rowing in the right direction. We'll also cover a few common pitfalls, so you'll know what to do if they happen to you. To accomplish this, we'll travel through four action-packed chapters together.

In "Chapter 10 – When & How to Recruit Your A-team or Love the Creatures You're With," we'll discuss how to identify who you need, how to evaluate whether you have the right team members, and how to start socializing the project to rally support. While the song lyric advice from Stephen Stills to "love the one you're with" is helpful when you have limited or no options regarding who is part of your project, you may have more influence than you think! We'll discuss how our animal avatars can help us create a winning team, and how to create your step-by-step plan to recruit your A-team and get them committed to win.

In "Chapter 11 – What to Do About Stakeholders, Especially the Difficult Ones," we'll further explore how to think about and identify who your stakeholders are and what to do about them. You'll learn how to organize stakeholders into three fun categories with the help of our animal avatars, as well as plan what to do next. You'll also meet SAMM, our related "thinking tool," which is part of our pro project management workbook that you can download for free from the Project Guru Press website (projectgurupress.com/meettheplayers/

tools). Many clients have found this thinking tool to be the key to success for their projects, and you might, too! As you know, everyone has an opinion, and these techniques can help you sort through and manage the noise.

In "Chapter 12 – Get Ready for the Storm: Teaming is a Process, Too," you'll learn one of the most surprising and frequent team traps and discover powerful tips for climbing out of it.

At this stage in the book, you'll have identified all the key players in your version of Projectland—those who you believe will help you achieve your objectives—and you'll know how to navigate any early team turmoil. Next, you'll learn how to ensure they're all in your project boat, in the right seats, and ready to row in the right direction.

In "Chapter 13 – Your Secret Weapon to Get the Players Rowing in the Same Direction," we'll review a simple, powerful pro technique to get your crew and project started successfully: how to prepare a solid, succinct kickoff meeting. Since sometimes the first secret weapon just isn't enough to get the team to push off the dock and start rowing, "Chapter 14 -- When Part One Isn't Enough," walks you through how to extend that kickoff meeting into a full-fledged, efficient planning workshop. And with this, you'll be in a solid position to embark on your project journey.

One last point worth mentioning before we get on our way. You may notice a few points being repeated throughout the book. This is because after you've read the book once, you may want to go back and use certain chapters as reference. By then, you may or may not have remembered key principles mentioned earlier in the book. For convenience (and, let's face it, to drill the point home), I reiterate certain crucial concepts throughout the book. While I try to keep it to a minimum, expect some minor repetition periodically.

Are you ready? I'll be your tour guide who attempts to make the journey fun. Let's lace up our hiking boots, grab some electrolyte water and energy bars, and get started. First, we'll sit at the start of the path for a minute, so that I can cover a few key pointers to make sure we're on the same page before we head into the wilderness.

It's time. You're ready. Welcome to the jungle.

SECTION ONE
WELCOME TO THE JUNGLE

First, let's cover key foundational concepts that you need to know before we can get to the "who's who" and meet the players.

CHAPTER 1
WHAT IS A PROJECT? WHAT IS NOT?

"It's a lack of clarity that
creates chaos and frustration.
Those emotions are poison to any living goal."
- Steve Maraboli, *Life, the Truth, and Being Free*[1]

DELAWARE – MAJOR HOSPITAL SYSTEM KICKOFF

As I begin the kickoff meeting, I look around the enormous conference room at seasoned, stoic, skeptical hospital administrators, while another delayed doctor rushes in the room and grabs a seat. It's our first time working with this prestigious group, and we're about to rock their project world.

I get a few minutes into my opening remarks, and a hand slowly goes up. "Can I ask a question," asks the respected administrator who has been working at this place for decades. "What is a project – really?"

I admit I stared at her in shock for a moment. I thought, "Wow. If this brilliant lady isn't confident in the answer to that, then I better start with this cornerstone from now on." After all, why start talking about project management, when not everyone is on the same page about what a project is and what a project is not?

WHAT IS A PROJECT – REALLY?

How confident are you in answering this question? In my workshops, I start with a *fill in the blank* exercise using the definition of a project from the Project Management Institute (PMI) and ask people to write down what they think the blanks are.

Why not give this exercise a whirl for yourself:

A project is a _____ endeavor,

undertaken to create a _____

product, _____, or result.

By the way, the majority of people get most, if not all, of the blanks wrong, so don't worry! You are in good company and learning something new.

Ready for the answers? According to PMI, a project is "a <u>temporary</u> endeavor undertaken to create a <u>unique</u> product, <u>service</u>, or result[2]." The words *temporary* and *unique* are of utmost importance in figuring out what constitutes a project and what does not.

Simply speaking, an organization does only two things: projects and operations. Some organizations may call operations by other terms, such as *maintenance, business as usual, keep the lights on,* and *run the engine.* For-profit companies, no matter what they sell, are in the business of making money. Operations are whatever they do every day to bring money in the door. They turn their special crank that makes the company money. Nonprofit or governmental organizations turn their own cranks that serve a purpose.

When operations does a good job, the cranks generate excess money that can be invested back in the organization so it can grow. And how do organizations typically grow? Projects!

YOU NEED THREE INGREDIENTS TO BAKE THIS CAKE

Remember, the first two key ingredients required for work to be defined as a project are that it is "temporary and unique." So, the purpose of a project may be to expand operations by adding another crank or figuring out how to make an existing crank permanently go faster.

Let's break down *temporary* and *unique* a bit further since it's so important.

Temporary references a definite start and end. Let's say you bought a new house and you want to host a large family holiday dinner. Is that a project? Let's figure it out.

First, is it temporary? Can you define a definite start and end? The *start* could be when you begin planning an elaborate holiday meal and decide to invite twenty family members. The *end* might be serving that meal successfully and restoring the household back to normal within twenty-four hours of the event. All the things done in the middle to make that happen include various tasks such as planning the meal, writing the list, checking it twice, traveling to the store, grocery shopping, unloading the groceries, cooking, cleaning the dishes, escorting family members out the door, and putting all the horribly uncomfortable fold-up metal chairs back in the basement. Whew! It's temporary because there is an end. Thank goodness. That was a lot of work!

Second, is it *unique*? Since it's the first time you've ever hosted an elaborate holiday meal in your new home, I'd say that makes it unique.

The question you need to ask to discover whether or not the work has the third ingredient is this: *Does it create a product, service, or result?* If so, then you have the third ingredient. For our elaborate holiday meal, I'd say family members with full bellies, fun photos, and, hopefully, happy holiday memories definitely count.

Have you ever heard someone say they are working on an "ongoing" project? That's as much of an oxymoron as "completely unfinished" or "accurate estimate." The word *ongoing* is a red flag because it tends to violate the *temporary* rule. If you have an "ongoing project," you need to evaluate whether it is really *operations*. One could argue that weekly shopping trips are part of operating the household and are therefore not projects, while someone else will argue that every trip to the store is a small project.

You may be wondering why it even matters what we call it. To-may-toe, to-mah-toe. Technically that's fair. But the main reason why we care to define when something is a project is to make sure we apply the skills, knowledge, tools, and techniques that will be helpful in ensuring that it is a success. Something that has become as routine as a weekly grocery shopping trip certainly feels different and requires less planning than hosting your first holiday meal for 20 people in your new home.

As far as *unique* goes, that can invite a great debate, too. Unique means, in the history of the world, this particular undertaking has never been done before; in this time, in this place, or with these people. SOMETHING makes it truly unique.

SPECIAL SITUATION: THE RECURRING PROJECT

During practically every speech where I've explained this, this is the point where an enthusiastic hand shoots up and shouts, "Yeah, but, what about the projects that we do over and over again?" Indeed, there are projects such as hosting an annual signature conference, creating the company's annual report, and publishing books. I call them *recurring* projects. They still fit the criteria. They are temporary —there is a definite beginning and end for each instance. There are aspects that make the project unique, such as the annual conference having a different theme, being hosted in a different city, or having different speakers and team members. And, the project creates a product, service, or result, or you shouldn't keep doing it over and over again. When advising corporations about recurring projects, we discuss what they need to do to create a *playbook* that reduces uncertainty in the areas that are similar, while also accommodating what makes the current project cycle unique. This additional deliverable ensures that the information about how this important work gets done is out of the heads of the resources and written into a plan.

Recurring projects are a different animal than day-to-day operations. If you have a recurring project on your plate, create a basic playbook as you go. Then, at the beginning of the next cycle you don't have to start from scratch. You can dust it off, and dive into confirming what is the same, changing the things that are unique, and evaluating the unique aspects for new risks and opportunities. This will accelerate your planning cycle, increase confidence, and make life easier when project team members change.

THE OPERATIONS SNIFF TEST

Let's return to the grocery store example for a moment, since my "I don't care what you call it" rant doesn't fly with people who like definitive answers. I personally would call weekly grocery shopping *operations* rather than a small project. For me, this is a joyless chore that I want to complete as quickly as possible. To help me get through it without losing my mind, I run the "meal planning/grocery shopping" crank the same way every time. I could write a Standard Operating Procedure (SOP) for how I do this.

Sure, the meals are unique and when the sale item I wanted is out of stock, it might throw a wrench in my meal plan for twenty seconds while I decide if I substitute it with something else or skip it. Risks and issues occur in operations too. The idea is to make the decisions or do the firefighting required and get back to running things smoothly as quickly as possible.

Here's the sniff test for whether something is definitely operations. If you sense that you can create an SOP and hand that SOP over to a lower cost resource to run, assuming they have or can learn the skills, then welcome to operations. In fact, the goal in operations is to turn the crank better, faster, and cheaper without the crank flying off its axle and hurting someone (safety first!).

THE FINAL "BRIDGE" BEFORE WE HEAD TO PROJECTLAND

Because learning to identify when you have a project (and/or knowing how to clearly define what you have as a project) is so critical to the rest of what we're going to explore together, let's wrap this up with one final point and illustration.

Even though a project is temporary, the goal of most projects is to create a unique and lasting outcome. Of course, if the project is not planned and executed properly, that may not be the inevitable result.

For example, if all goes well when building a bridge, the result will be a strong, dependable structure that allows people to cross a body of water safely. Every bridge is unique. Aspects such as the depth of the water, exact length of the bridge, the type of bridge, the building crew, and the municipalities on either side of the bridge, can all contribute to making the project unique.

While the process of building a bridge is temporary, the result is a lasting structure that then needs to be maintained properly. And who does the maintenance? Operations!

CONCLUSION

Your first job is to recognize what is a project and what is operations.

And remember, a project is a temporary endeavor undertaken to create a unique product, service, or result. If you have all three of these ingredients required to bake this cake (i.e., unique, temporary, and creates a product, service, or result), then you have a project on your plate. Feel confident that you can use project management skills, tools, and techniques to deliver successful outcomes and maybe even have a little fun along the way too.

WHAT'S NEXT?

Now that we're clear on what a project is and what it's not, it's time to welcome you to Projectland. You'll discover why I call it Projectland and what it means for you. We'll dive deeper into what makes the world of projects and the world of operations different, and why understanding the rules of Projectland is critical to your career.

At the end of each section, I'll provide some ideas for how you can apply what you've learned to your job. For those of you who like a challenge, enjoy!

PRACTICAL PROJECTLAND CHALLENGE

I hope you now feel more confident that you know the difference between projects and operations. What will you do with what you've learned?

Take Action!

1. Listen for the word "ongoing." I hear it a lot in all the law enforcement shows I watch, when they say, "ongoing investigation." When I hear "ongoing project," my ears perk up and a lighthearted interrogation begins to determine whether the project was poorly defined, it should be treated as a recurring project, or it's really operations.

2. Think about your goals at work or at home, and what is operations vs. projects. How can you use the tips in this chapter to make operations work better, faster, or cheaper? How can you define your project work so that the three ingredients are crystal clear?

3. Think about one thing on your plate right now that you're not entirely sure is a project or operations. Remember, you can figure out if your work is a project by checking to see if you have all three ingredients:

- Temporary – it has a definite start and end,
- Unique – no one has ever done this before (e.g., in this time, in this place, with these people), and
- Creates a product, service, or result.

Go ahead, give it a try!

CHAPTER 2
WELCOME TO PROJECTLAND

"With a tree, all the growth
takes place at the growing tips.
Humanity is exactly the same.
All the growth takes place in the growing tip:
among that one percent of the population.
It's made up of pioneers, the beginners.
That's where the action is."
- Abraham Maslow[1]

"Projects are DIFFERENT. It's like a whole different world. Perhaps we should call it... *Projectland*," I blurted out to the wide-eyed group of adult learners.

About a week after the training, I returned to the client's office and was walking down the hall on the way to see the executive who hired us to help her team up their game. They were all great at operations, but they were new to projects and new to her. And let me tell you, this lady was sharp: an Ivy League MBAer, bilingual, a former electrical engineer, and a terrific leader who I'd worked with in the past.

I had just walked past two of the gents who were in the training class. As I was caught up in my own head, I didn't hear the conversation as I walked by and waved. But the next comment made me stop in my tracks. "Remember, it's different. It's Projectland."

After years of trying to explain to colleagues, then clients, then audiences, why projects are DIFFERENT, I finally bumbled, stumbled, and landed on the answer in one word. Thanks to the advice of my Book Insider VIPs (my inner circle of beta readers), I settled on depicting it with the capital "P" like Philadelphia, so that it feels like a real place. We call it *Projectland*.

Welcome to the world of projects, dear reader! I've now been calling it Projectland for many years, because it does seem to help everyone from executives to college students quickly appreciate that the project world is completely different from the world of operations. It's a different environment with different rules, just as Earth has gravity and astronauts have to learn to operate without it to go to the moon. Many successful and experienced people assume that the same rules that have worked well for them for decades in operations will also work on a project. Trust me when I say that this can be a disruptive or even disastrous assumption.

How is it different?

Here's an example. Have you ever heard a boss say, "don't bring me a problem without a solution?" This advice can backfire in Projectland. Project managers need to WELCOME problems and encourage team members to share them immediately. Why? Those problems might just delay the entire project, especially if a team member feels they can't bring a problem forward without having a solution ready.

As we explored in the previous chapter, projects, by definition, are temporary and unique. Since part of the definition is that it is unique, this means that you and your team are PIONEERS headed across unknown territory, whereas operations mostly deals in familiar terrain. Of course, in either case, there will be obstacles that you haven't seen before and aren't sure how to overcome. What's great about Projectland is that you often get to work as part of a team.

"There has to be this pioneer, the individual who has the courage, the ambition to overcome the obstacles that always develop when one tries to do something worthwhile, especially when it is new and different."[2]

– ALFRED P. SLOAN

When I worked in technology operations, my boss called us a team, but it felt more like a group of individual contributors doing related work. A project team, particularly one that is motivated, feels like a unit, because the group is united in a journey to achieve a goal. I felt this way playing sports and music. We all have our assigned positions, and need each other to do our best every day.

Teamwork DOES make the dream work in Projectland because when an unidentified creature jumps out and surprises a team member who's not sure how to respond, they can ask for help. Don't be surprised if a colleague has encountered this creature or one of its cousins on some other project and can make helpful suggestions.

Let's talk about the terrain of Projectland a bit. Here are five more examples that may help you figure out if you are living in or visiting Projectland or Operations. Many modern workers are hired to do a day job (operations), and then a project lands on their laps. If this happens to you, consider it a strong vote of confidence in your abilities!

Projects	Operations
Temporary - A schedule is developed based on how long it will take to deliver the product, service or result expected. Decisions often need to be made to either stay on time or to extend the timeline.	**Ongoing** - This is your "day job." The schedule is usually based on a "normal" work day.
Budget is expected to be finite and closed when the *temporary* project is complete.	**Budget** is usually annual, and a profit is expected.
Resources are pulled together to get the project done. When a resource on the project leaves, it can be enormously disruptive to the project.	**Resources** are hired and may do the same job for years. You may hear, "everyone is replaceable", because Standard Operating Procedures (SOPs) can be created and repeatedly followed with confidence.
The main goal is to deliver the product, service or result on time, on budget, on scope, on quality with a high degree of stakeholder satisfaction.	**The main goal** is often to drive down the cost of operations while increasing profit margin.
Unique - In the history of the world, no one has ever done this before (e.g., in this time, in this place, with these people), which means that the entire endeavor tends to be risky, and success is not at all certain.	The whole point of operations is that it **runs continuously**. When stuff happens that disrupts business, it can be a bit like firefighting, including a lot of stress until the smoke clears.

Table 2.1 – Comparing Projects and Operations

Projectland looks and feels a little different to everyone because we each look at the terrain through our unique binoculars. Our views have been formed from our experience, culture, industry, company, department, and so on.

Let's explore three typical elements that fall under the heading *workplace culture*, that will help you define your version of Projectland. Workplace culture is definitely something that you need to understand to be successful, because it can influence how people behave and respond to typical requests by project leaders. The three characteristics that can make a big difference to how Projectland feels and how effective you can be are: *risk tolerance, organizational authority*, and *action-results orientation*. For each of these, there can be a wide range of experiences. The unwritten rules of engagement of what is typically acceptable and unacceptable will generally be directly correlated to where your organization sits on the spectrum. Let's examine these in more detail.

THREE TYPICAL PROJECTLAND PITFALLS

Does your organization encourage people to take risks in their work? Are people punished in some way if they take a risk and it doesn't work out the way they'd hoped? In working with governmental organizations, I discovered that they tend to have low risk tolerance because they're highly susceptible to media scrutiny. It makes sense that decisions require a lot of people and take a lot longer than at a social media software company that values speed and figures that they can always course correct by making another decision later.

Risk tolerance is one of the elements to watch out for in Projectland. It is woven into the fabric of your workplace culture, and understanding where yours falls on the spectrum can help you operate in tune with what is generally acceptable. It can also help you be intentional about influencing the organization to adopt a different risk assessment process in order to achieve its desired project goals.

The next one is *organizational authority,* i.e., how people are organized and authorized to get work done. For example, one of the complaints I often hear in cultures where there are consequences if one breaks the "chain of command," is that project managers don't have authority. In these cultures, project managers need to be clearly empowered by senior leaders, otherwise people will continue to go to their direct managers for guidance even though those managers don't —and shouldn't—know the day-to-day project details.

The other end of the spectrum is an organization that is highly *projectized*. At one such client, they had a well-defined process for authorizing projects, selecting the team, and creating a special workspace for them. They had a facilities team that quickly set up temporary walls, an office for the project sponsor, a conference table, cubes for team leads, and big worktables for team members. The workspace was arranged in a way that isolated full-time project leaders and team members from the rest of the organization so that they could focus.

In any case, whether your project is being undertaken in a hierarchical maze of reporting structures, a neatly isolated oasis with its own resources, or somewhere in between, you'll need to know which terrain you're operating in. Otherwise, you could break a rule or step on a sensitive soul's toes without realizing it.

The third potential pitfall is how *action- and results-oriented* the culture is. There tends to be a spectrum here too. Consider which of the following descriptions is the closest match for your world, and the corresponding actions that you might take to influence the culture.

- *All planning, no action.* This is also known as *analysis paralysis* – we don't actually do anything; we just talk a lot about doing things. In this environment, you usually need to make it safe to take even a small action so that results can be experienced. This helps with forward momentum. Aim for a quick, safe win. And then another. And another.
- *Action, but no progress.* The wheels are spinning, but the car isn't going anywhere. Often, the root of this is perfectionism or fear. To paraphrase Voltaire: Don't let perfect be the enemy of good. Choose "good" and get going!
- *All action, no planning.* It feels like go, go, go! Get going, somewhere, anywhere, NOW! This often results in a feeling of panic, chaos, and going in the wrong direction. Get ready for some annoying rework or make it safe to plan. Typically, people start running around because they're afraid of not looking busy. Consider emphasizing that planning *is* doing, and doing planning is an important part of ensuring that we figure out how to efficiently get to the goal together.
- Closer to a *healthy balance* between the extremes. In our consulting engagements, we look to help the organization move toward a *healthy culture that gets results*, where there is "just enough" planning to ensure the right action is taken and wasteful rework is avoided. If this describes where you work, consider yourself fortunate and support the balance.

If you're wondering how to organize everyone in the beginning of the project, stay tuned for Section III. For now, note how a different approach can be taken based on the type of culture, to either influence the organization toward or to maintain a healthy culture that gets results.

In addition to these three aspects, there can be countless characteristics that make up your version of Projectland. However, there are probably just a few key factors that are core to understanding the rules and expectations in your world. Just like in any game, once you understand what the rules are, you can more easily create your gameplan to win.

WHAT'S NEXT?

Now that you know what a project is and I've welcomed you to Projectland, you may be wondering how to navigate this world like a pro. While there is such a creature as a professional project manager, which we'll explore when we meet the players in Section II, let's step back for a moment. Because when people hear I'm in the project management business, I almost always get asked: *Is project management just like management?* Let's explore the answer to this next, which is the final leg of our journey through the foundational concepts in welcoming you to the jungle.

PRACTICAL PROJECTLAND CHALLENGE

Explore the concept of Projectland in your world.
Take Action!

1. Throughout your day, notice what work you do is a project and what is ongoing operations (often also known as your "day job"). To help you with this exercise, if you haven't already done so, review the previous section called "What is a project? What is not?"

2. Observe, talk to people at your workplace whom you respect, and write down the characteristics you feel make up the terrain of YOUR version of Projectland. For example, what does the risk tolerance, orga-

nizational authority, and action-results orientation look like in your organization? And which of the action-results descriptions we discussed is the closest match for your world?

- All planning, no action
- Action, but no progress
- All action, no planning
- A healthy balance

3. Get ready for an exciting ride!

CHAPTER 3
IS PROJECT MANAGEMENT JUST LIKE MANAGEMENT?

"Managers light a fire under people;
leaders light a fire in people."
- Kathy Austin[1]

While leading a team of professional project managers in the Fortune 500, an experienced colleague came to me and complained that not all of our project managers were the same. I asked what she meant exactly. She said one was direct and serious, another was happy and collaborative, and others were in between. I asked, "Do you feel confident that the project managers can lead their respective projects to victory?" She said, "Yes, but something still isn't right. Aren't they all supposed to do it the same way?"

The answer is yes and no. Project management is an art and a science. Yes, all of the project managers need to do the science in a similar way, because otherwise it would feel like chaos to team members on multiple projects. AND no matter what project manager a team member gets, they should understand the language the project manager is using and what's expected of them. I asked, "Do you agree that art is subjective? That the art I like may not be the art you like, but neither of us is wrong?" She crinkled her face and replied, "Yes." The art part is the person's unique leadership style, and everyone has a leadership style they prefer. Some people like Jack Welch and some prefer Mother Teresa.

On our team, I was thrilled that every project manager had a different set of experiences and leadership styles. First, because I never want anyone to feel like they have to pretend to be someone they're not. That just takes too much energy and Projectland is already very demanding. Second, because every project is unique, I like to match the project to the style of project manager that it needs.

For instance, for the project that absolutely had to get done on time no matter what, I assigned the project manager whose style was more like a hammer. She was highly skilled at pushing through tough situations over and over again. The project that included some sensitive souls and required more diplomacy, I assigned to the project manager whose style was more like WD40. Meaning, he can get along with virtually anyone, and his superpower was getting everything to run smoothly despite the variety of personalities involved.

Third, project sponsors also have their own leadership styles, and they need to get along with their project managers. And, the project managers need to get along with them. If everyone were the same, we'd be in big trouble trying to navigate all these variables. My colleague walked away with a new appreciation for project management as both an art and a science. While, yes, *project management* is the term we all use, in some ways the more accurate term is *project leadership* because it emphasizes that *leadership* is what project managers do.

LEADERS, PROJECT MANAGERS, AND MANAGERS – OH MY!

Now we've introduced another term, *leadership*. Believe it or not, project management, leadership, and management are three different animals. Did I say animals? This is bananas!

Let's step back. What's the difference between leadership and management? As Kathy Austin explains in the chapter's introductory quote, "Managers light a fire under people. Leaders light a fire in people." Furthermore, when Marcus Buckingham spoke at the Inc. Magazine and Winning Workplaces Leadership Conference to an audience of Chief Executive Officers (CEOs), he explained that leadership is the opposite of management, the roles are fundamentally different and, "Very few of you will be very, very good at both."

And this, my ambitious friend, is a big challenge in Projectland. He goes on to explain that "Modern day leaders traffic in the unknown," and their challenge is to "take people's legitimate anxiety about the unknown and turn it into confidence, into spiritedness." Meanwhile a manager's role is to "get people to work harder for you than they would for someone else."[2]

So, neither leadership nor management is sufficient to conquer Projectland. We need both. We need people who can continuously motivate a team to work really, really hard toward a goal—a team that probably has never worked together before—ALL while in Projectland, which is, by definition, unknown territory. Enter project management, and why I'd rather call it project leadership.

Leaders, project managers, and managers are all important roles, and not everyone is built to be all three. Based on your strengths, you may find one to be a better fit than the others, and that's great! Since we're in Projectland, let's dive deeper into what project management is.

❧

PROJECT MANAGEMENT: THE ART & SCIENCE

It stands to reason that when you're working on a project, you'll benefit from using practical project management techniques to make sure it's a success. Regular "management" will not be enough, as we've just explored. This is why many people who have been successful in operations for years fail in Projectland. They assume the same rules that they've used to successfully navigate the operations world will work in Projectland. But what's the difference?

The Association for Project Management (APM) based in the United Kingdom explains: "A key factor that distinguishes project management from just 'management' is that it has this final deliverable and a **finite timespan**, unlike management which is an ongoing process."[3]

Getting anyone to do anything on time can be a challenge. It is even more of a challenge to get a group of people to get something done TOGETHER on time. A greater challenge still is getting a group of people to get something done together on time that THEY HAVE NEVER DONE BEFORE. This is why **project management is its own art and science**!

The science part of project management includes the proven, practical techniques that professional project managers apply. The art is about your own unique style for leading people into the wilderness of Projectland. Project people are pioneers. Project sponsors, steering teams, project managers, and team leads must be courageous leaders, because there are always obstacles to overcome as you move through the intense terrain of Projectland. Project management is a vehicle that can help teams reach their unique, tangible objectives with less stress in a finite period of time. The more people that are needed to accomplish the objectives, the more complicated and stressful the project work tends to get.

YOUR SECRET WEAPON AT WORK & IN LIFE

Project management can truly be your secret weapon to successfully deliver projects. That's why I love project management so much, and why I think more people should care to learn and apply it not only on the job, but also in their personal lives! It is indeed a skill that will help you succeed in work and in life, too!

Whether you're finding your first apartment, buying a home, moving to a new city, planning an epic vacation, or creating your side hustle, project management skills will help you accomplish more and stress less.

WHAT'S NEXT?

Great job wrapping up Section I! You've learned key fundamental concepts and started to consider what makes your project and your version of Projectland unique. Now you're ready to meet the players in Projectland, with the help of a fun assortment of animal avatars.

PRACTICAL PROJECTLAND CHALLENGE

What will you do with what you learned?

Take Action!

1. If you haven't read the introductory chapter where I explain the not so fun fact about most projects failing and a key reason being lack of proper management support, take a few minutes to do that now. Then, reflect on scenario(s) where a lack of management support has led to failure. If you are new to an organization, identify someone who can give you a history lesson, and ask them if they've ever seen this happen in your organization.
2. Observe where you see differences between management, leadership and project management.
3. Observe where you see art and where you see science being applied in getting projects done.
4. Observe different leadership styles and note what you like and would like to emulate as well as what you don't like so that you can develop your own unique project leadership style. Remember that even if you're not in a leadership role, you can lead by influence, as intern Sebastian illustrated in the opening chapter when he asked a few intelligent questions.

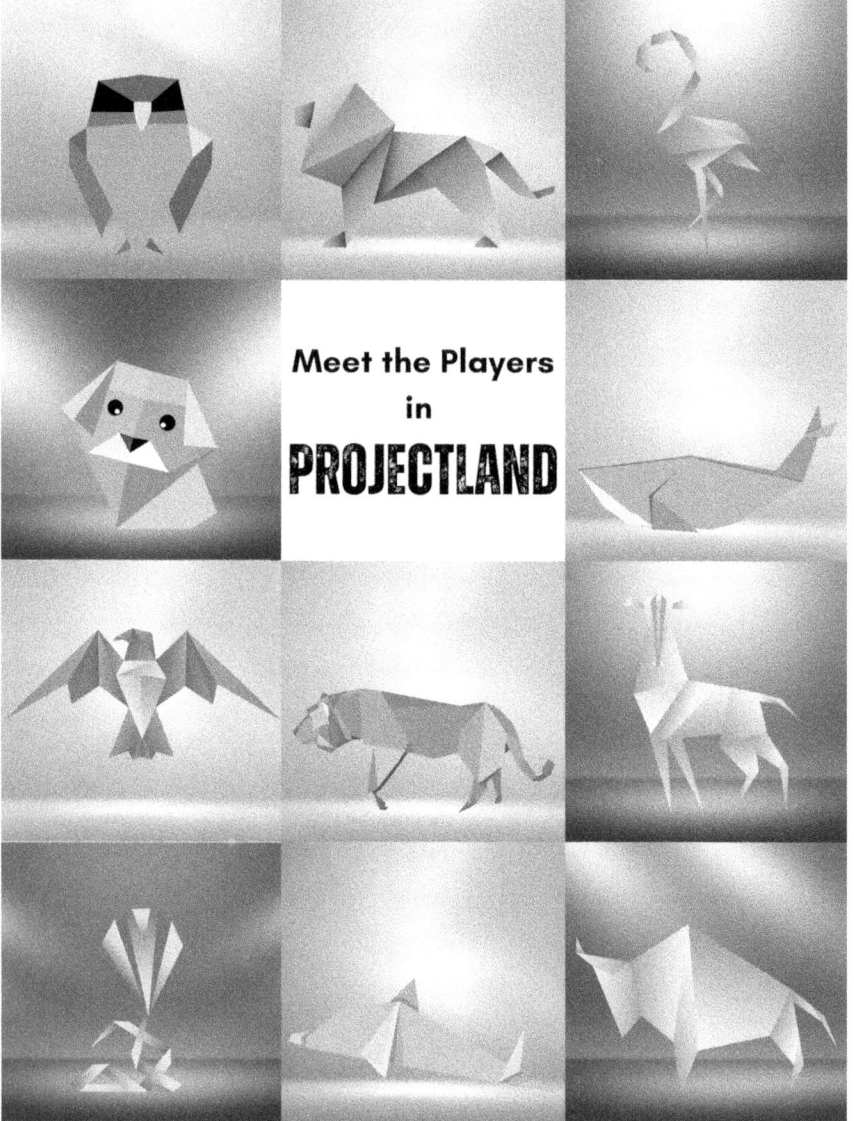

Meet the Players
in
PROJECTLAND

SECTION TWO
MEET THE PLAYERS

Introducing the typical who's who in Projectland with the help of carefully curated animal avatars.

CHAPTER 4
WHO'S WHO IN PROJECTLAND

"We have more to learn from animals
than animals have to learn from us."
- Anthony D. Williams, Author

To play basketball, you need to learn that one of the five people on the court is called the "point guard," and it's usually not the biggest, tallest person. If you are choosing your team members for soccer and hockey, you know you need someone who is a really good goalie or you're in trouble. If you're in the orchestra, there's a first chair and a second chair, and the flute players (flautists) all sit together. You get the point. Every team effort tends to have its own language and roles with specific responsibilities and desirable characteristics. The same is true in Projectland.

A project can be a great experience when everyone involved knows their role, feels that they can be successful in it, and understands what to expect from everyone else. Defining project roles and setting responsibility expectations makes it easier for teams to learn to work well together and row in the same direction to meet the project's objectives.

If even one person on a white-water raft isn't performing well in their role, the boat can capsize, making everyone cold, wet, and upset.

So, let's make sure that we have a common understanding of all the roles that may be needed on a project, what they can expect from one another, and how they are organized.

TYPICAL PROJECTLAND REPORTING STRUCTURE

Since every project is unique, we need to take some time to determine who the right people are and how to best organize them to achieve the project's goals.

For the project to be successful it often has a reporting structure like the one in figure 4.1. Note that the descriptions that follow are meant to provide a brief introduction, and you will learn even more about each role in the following chapters. Keep in mind that not all of these roles make sense for every project, and your organization may use different terminology.

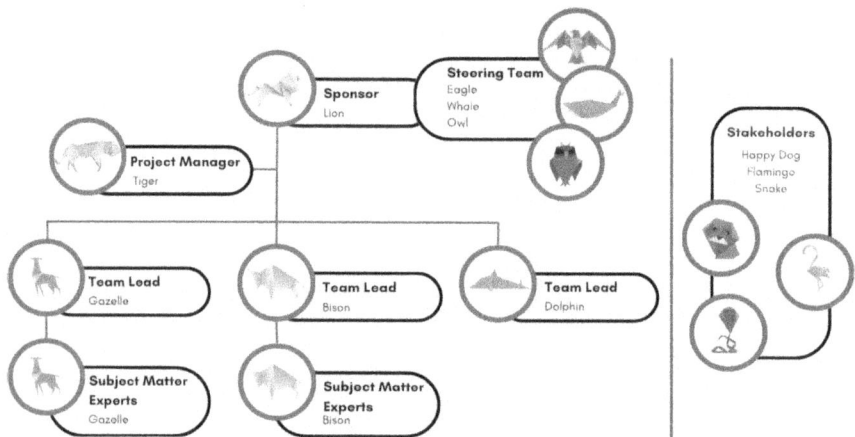

Figure 4.1 - Typical Projectland Reporting Structure

A project team is comprised of Subject Matter Experts (SMEs) and project leaders.

The SMEs do the work of the project, such as creating the product, service, or result, and getting the humans ready for the change the project brings. Many times, the SMEs don't self-identify as experts, and that's okay! By the end of the project, they will know more about the topic than anyone else in the organization.

The superset of project leaders includes the sponsor, steering team, project manager, and team leads. Not every project has all these roles. Project leaders provide direction and support to the SMEs, such as clearing roadblocks, making timely decisions, and garnering support for the project throughout the organization.

Everyone else who cares about the project is considered a stakeholder.

Wait...What? Doesn't the team have a stake in the project too? Absolutely! But to keep it simple, we'll refer only to the people who are *outside* of the project team as stakeholders from now on.

The Project Management Institute defines a stakeholder as *an individual, group, or organization that may affect, be affected by, or perceive itself to be affected by a decision, activity, or outcome of a project, program, or portfolio.*[1]

WHEW! Yes, I agree that was a mouthful, and I had to read that many times over until I really understood it. Here's my simplified translation. *Stakeholders can love your project, hate your project, or be somewhere in between.* In fact, it can be helpful to categorize stakeholders as cheerleaders, saboteurs, or finicky fans and then manage them accordingly. (More on how to do that in "Chapter 9: Three Surprising Kinds of Stakeholders.")

BRIEF INTRODUCTION TO THE ROLES & ANIMAL AVATARS

Throughout this book, we will use animal avatars to represent the various characters in Projectland. It makes them easier to remember and adds a bit of fun.

Continuing our conversation about stakeholders, let's talk about the three types and their corresponding, carefully curated, animal avatars.

The Cheerleader – Our animal avatar for a stakeholder who is a cheerleader for your project is the happy dog. Yes, cheerleaders are great to have around, just like happy dogs. My dog is especially happy when I'm cooking, because she knows I'm going to drop something on the floor. But, it's no good when she's underfoot! On projects, it's similar. We need to make sure we harness the cheerleaders' energy for good, and they don't accidentally cause issues.

The Saboteur – Let's explore saboteurs next. Can you guess which creature represents these stakeholders? If you said the snake, you're right! (With a friendly shout out and all due respect to the serpentologists out there.) If you don't identify where the potential saboteurs are for your project, they could jump out of the weeds and surprise you with a lethal bite. At first, some newbies have a hard time believing that anyone inside their organization could be a saboteur, because we're all supposed to be on the same team, right? Right, and unfortunately, there are still people that will not be supportive, and in fact may work against you on purpose or accidentally. It's best to stop and think about who this might be, rather than be surprised later.

The Finicky Fan – In between those cheerleaders and saboteurs are the finicky fans, which are represented by the flamingo. Flamingos must be finicky with their diets to retain their vibrant color, and they tend to flock and squawk together. After twenty years living and breathing Philadelphia sports fandom, I have definitely met a few finicky fans. These folks sit on the fence, waiting to see how things are going before picking a side. We need to move them into the cheering section as quickly as possible and keep them away from the saboteurs.

The Team – Now that we've introduced the three surprising types of stakeholders, let's dive into the project team roles. We'll start with the project sponsor at the top of Figure 4.1, which shows the Typical Projectland Reporting Structure.

The Project Sponsor – The top leader of the project is the sponsor. The sponsor is often the person who provides the financial resources, in cash or in kind, for the project, or is the representative of the group who does.

In the animal kingdom, the sponsor is like the lion. When the lion roars, ALLLLL of the creatures are on edge. When the lion is calm, the creatures can casually go about their business.

Sometimes you'll hear something like "finance is sponsoring the project." This does NOT mean that we encourage management by committee. In fact, we insist on ONE person being the sponsor who is best suited to make decisions and invest the time required to be a positive steward. Having more than one sponsor is impractical, slows things down, and makes the project manager's job infinitely more difficult and complex. There can only be one king or queen of the jungle, after all. Any other candidates for the sponsor role can be on the steering team.

The Steering Team – If a steering team is created, it is usually because additional leaders are needed to assist the sponsor in ensuring success of cross-functional, large, highly visible, complex, risky, or geographically dispersed projects. We prefer to call this group a *team* rather than a *committee* to emphasize that we do NOT manage projects by committee. The chair of the steering team is the sponsor. The lion can't see the terrain from up above or know what's happening in the sea, and needs good advice, especially in dark times, to make decisions. Steering Team members are like eagles, whales, and owls—allowing visibility from above, below, and in the dark, respectively. If your project does not need a steering team, GREAT! Don't force it. If it does need one, GREAT. But get ready to up your game because your performance will be even more visible.

The Project Manager – This is the person responsible for the success of a project, in charge of all aspects of it, and who reports to the sponsor. The tiger is our animal avatar. Tigers are not quite the king or queen of the jungle, but awfully close. Many times, project managers need to harness the courage and fierceness of the big cat to do all the things that good leaders do.

The Team Lead – Team lead is a typical role needed for geographically dispersed, technically complex, or larger projects. Team leads are often subject matter experts who coordinate the work of fellow experts to plan and create project deliverables. Team leads report to the project manager. Just like there are a few elder, alpha animals in a herd, team leads tend to be experienced and respected leaders in their areas of expertise.

Team members or Subject Matter Experts (SMEs) – Team members may be from different groups with knowledge of a specific subject matter or with a specific skillset who carry out the work of the project. Team members report to the team lead, if that role exists, or directly to the project manager. In the animal kingdom, great team players with special skills include the *bison, gazelle,* and *dolphin.* Later, we'll dive much deeper into the characteristics of these animal avatars and explore why they can help us select the right mix of skills and strengths to help our projects be successful.

Now that you know the players, you can better determine where you fit and what to expect from everyone else. And with everyone feeling confident in their roles, working well together and appreciating each other's contributions to the project, don't be surprised if you have a little fun too.

WHAT'S NEXT?

I hope you had fun learning the players in Projectland with the help of our animal avatar introductions. The remaining chapters in this section are dedicated to diving more deeply into each of the players, so that you can learn even more about what is typically expected of them, how to be great, and avoid common pitfalls. We'll start by exploring the role of Project Sponsor shown at the top of Figure 4.1, because this is the boss on the project who sets the tone, can drive the project over a cliff, or be key to its success.

PRACTICAL PROJECTLAND CHALLENGE

What will you do with what you've learned?

Take Action!

1. Self-assess and look around! Which animal avatar characteristics do you feel you embody? Need a cheat sheet? Check out Appendix C or get the fun infographic from the Project Guru Press website (projectgurupress.com/meettheplayers/tools)

2. How about your team? Think about your projects. Who's who and where do you fit?

3. If you're the project manager, harness your inner tiger and make "who's who" clear. You can use the worksheet available at the Project Guru Press website (projectgurupress.com/meettheplayers/tools) to help you draft a business-friendly diagram to share with your project sponsor and get feedback.

4. If who's who is not clear in your version of Projectland, keep reading!

CHAPTER 5
I'M THE SPONSOR, HEAR ME ROAR

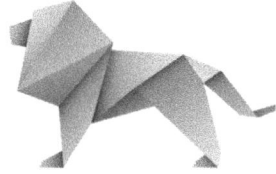

"I am certain that one bad general is better than two good ones."
- Napoleon Bonaparte, Emperor

My eyes went wide; I rapidly blinked, and gulped, all in quick succession. Did I hear that right? Did the CEO in front of me just declare, "I need one throat to choke!?" After a quick rewind in my mind, I concluded that yes... YES, he really said that.

The good news about this violent, inappropriate-for-the-modern-workplace comment, is that it does illustrate the first cardinal rule of defining the leadership team for your project. There can only be ONE person who is assigned as the project sponsor, and they don't need to be a top-level executive.

As mentioned earlier, the sponsor is often the person who provides the financial resources, in cash or in kind, for the project, or is the representative of the group who does. The sponsor should be the leader who is best suited to make decisions and invest the time required to be a positive steward. Having more than one sponsor is impractical, slows things down, and makes the project manager's job infinitely more difficult and unnecessarily complex. Any other candidates for the sponsor role can be on the steering team.

WHAT LIONS & PROJECT SPONSORS HAVE IN COMMON

Our animal avatar for the sponsor role is the lion. There can only be one king (or queen!) of the jungle, after all. When the lion is calm and happy, all the creatures in Projectland can go about their business with less stress. When the lion roars, everyone is on edge. Usually there is a good reason for the ruckus, though! Don't be surprised if the lion gets a little prickly when there are issues that should have been prevented, because the lion likes to see that everything is under control. Lions are known for their courage, and project sponsors must have the courage to stand up for their team, protect them from outside threats, and make unpopular decisions.

The sponsor is also like the owner of a sports team who sits up in the luxury box and makes the big decisions. In contrast, the project manager is like the head coach on the field. The sponsor's role is incredibly important. Sponsors need to show up, be accessible, and know enough about the details to be helpful while not meddling in day-to-day activities.

This can be a tricky balance for people new to this kind of leadership role, because most sponsors have become successful by being great at operations. They often don't realize that to be a great project sponsor, they need to understand that they are in Projectland now, which has different rules. For example, they may think they are making a simple suggestion that then inadvertently kicks off an entire tangent of work, distracting team members from agreed-upon pressing items. In operations, it might be a normal part of the day to make an improvement suggestion and have the team research it while the operational cranks continue to turn. In Projectland, this tends not to work, because we need to shield the team from distractions so that they can stay on task and on time. A sponsor's lack of awareness of how Projectland works can result in their becoming their own project's worst nightmare.

We have seen far too many sponsors unknowingly harm their projects, and then watch stressed out project managers perform damage control that could have been avoided. Time is money, and here in Projectland, we have schedules and budgets to manage. Poor sponsors can wreak havoc on projects when they cause extra work like this, because in Projectland, like life, there never seems to be enough time or money.

Our job in the beginning of the project is to identify one strong project sponsor. If the sponsor has already been identified and we are afraid that they will *not* be strong, we need to figure out how to surround them with people who can carry them through the tough terrain of Projectland. For instance, strong steering team members and a strong project manager can help offset sponsor weaknesses.

HOW DOES SOMEONE BECOME A PROJECT SPONSOR?

Sometimes an executive naturally assumes the role because she has an idea that she'd like to see come to life. Other times, some external factor (e.g., the government, a competitor, a disaster) forces a company to react and no executive really wants to devote the time to it, so they delegate it to an emerging leader as an "opportunity."

Whatever the situation, it's true that one reliable leader at the right level of the organization is needed to guide the project through its entire journey: from start to finish and even beyond, when the product, service, or result delivered by the project becomes the fabric of the way the organization operates moving forward.

**Sponsoring is a "full contact" sport
from start to finish and beyond.**

**However, the sponsor is the team owner,
not the head coach on the field.**

WHAT DOES A GREAT PROJECT SPONSOR DO?

Remember: Sponsoring is a **"full contact" sport** from start to finish and beyond. However, the sponsor **is the team owner, not the head coach on the field**. Specifically, what great sponsors do depends on the stage their project is in: in the beginning, throughout the project, at the end, and even beyond. Let's unpack each stage.

In the beginning...

When a project is first conceived, the sponsor champions the project to get it approved. This includes playing a significant role in developing the business case/cost justification and/or charter and leading the project through the engagement or selection process until it is formally authorized. It is a best practice to do this definition work, even if the sponsor has the sole authority to approve a project. The sponsor serves as the top spokesperson to higher levels of management, gathering support throughout the organization and promoting and articulating the benefits that the project will bring. If needed, the sponsor recruits the right leaders to be on the steering team.

Throughout the project...

Great sponsors accept that "stuff happens" on projects and stay calm. For issues that are beyond the control of the project manager, the sponsor serves as an escalation path. The sponsor should be involved in important decisions and events, such as thoughtfully authorizing changes in scope, actively participating in phase-end reviews, making sure the project is on track to provide the promised benefits, and making go/no-go decisions. A visible, engaged sponsor is helpful and necessary, especially when risks are particularly high.

If there is a steering team, the sponsor chairs it. Aligned with the infamous 80/20 rule, the sponsor should be able to make about 80% of the decisions. When the sponsor needs help to make the remaining 20% of the decisions, because the matter involves a topic outside of their expertise or authority, the sponsor calls upon steering team members to assist. Good sponsors proactively communicate the final decision to the project manager per the project schedule.

At the end...

Everything that was done earlier in the project was to prepare everyone for final delivery of the project's product, service, and/or result, and to set the organization up to achieve the benefits promised in the beginning. Sponsors play a key role in helping the organization strike a balance between pushing through to the end even if things aren't entirely perfect—OR having the courage to stop barreling toward the end when what you are likely facing is a cliff. Thelma & Louise is now considered a classic movie, but that literal cliffhanger ending was painful to watch, and not the kind of dramatic conclusion you want for your project!

Beyond...

As part of the project, we should have created a plan to measure and drive the benefits that the project promised. The proactive project manager may ensure that the first check-in report on benefits is scheduled after project delivery, as part of what's often called a "benefits realization" process. Many times, the sponsor becomes responsible for driving those benefits on an ongoing basis as part of operations. For instance, if new software is released, a key metric to track and report on could be *Adoption by Department*.

Let's summarize what a project sponsor does with our top ten list of responsibilities.

THE ONE PROJECT SPONSOR'S TOP 10 TYPICAL RESPONSIBILITIES

1. Provide the majority of project funding, in cash or kind
2. Gather support for the project and promote its benefits
3. Visibly lead as the top spokesperson
4. Set the direction and ensure successful delivery
5. Recruit the steering team (if appropriate) and chair meetings
6. Make about 80% of key decisions beyond the control of the project manager and engage the steering team as appropriate for the other 20%
7. Clear roadblocks
8. Advise the project manager on anything that is external to the project that might impact its success (e.g., cultural norms, geopolitical impacts, marketplace fluctuations, changes in organizational priorities or leadership, etc.)
9. Review progress on a regular basis and support ruthless, but thoughtful, management of change
10. Ensure a benefits realization plan is in place and that someone is assigned to continue to lead benefits realization after the project is complete

While all of this probably sounds like common sense, it isn't common knowledge or commonly embraced. I've seen super smart and savvy executive sponsors make major mistakes that in some cases have been fodder for media headlines and cost them their jobs.

But, by naming the role formally and keeping in mind that there are different things to focus on throughout the project lifecycle, you can go a long way to making sure that "lack of management support" isn't the reason your project failed.

That said, not every sponsor is created equal. I bet you have worked with or heard about leaders who have caused royal headaches for their people. In Projectland, pitfalls tend to be exacerbated.

In our classes, to make learning fun, we talk about good and evil behaviors. Let's face it, the "mean girls" and bullies who challenged us in childhood, grew up and went to work. But not all of them grew smarter or more compassionate.

Here are some of the evil project sponsor behaviors we've experienced, and what to do instead. This section's illustrations and tips are addressed directly to project sponsors who wish to become an appreciated sponsor and avoid common pitfalls.

EVIL SPONSOR #1 – THE "DRIVE BY" DIRECTION GIVER

We know you're a busy person, project sponsor. But the "drive-by" method results in bodies jumping around just like drive-by shootings do in action movies. Stopping someone in the hallway while you're running to a meeting or briefly standing in the doorway of your project manager's office for a moment, while hammering instructions without enough time for clarifying questions, a short discussion about priorities, or an understanding of context, is unfair. The result of a "drive-by" is generally either more disruptive than you imagined, or your request will be ignored until your direction is clear. Many projects have failed because the project manager was either too intimidated to ask qualifying or challenging questions of the sponsor, or wasn't afforded the opportunity. Don't foster such an environment.

Instead, plan for a 15-minute sit down, share the problem you are trying to solve and your ideas for how to solve it. Then stop and listen. Observe if there is squirming. Even if there is no visible seat-shifting reaction, it is likely that the project manager is imagining all of the implications to the work in progress. Ask about impact. Listen. Encourage questions. Beware of people just telling you what they think you want to hear. You do not want to become the emperor with no clothes.

EVIL SPONSOR #2 – THE VALLEY OF INDECISION DWELLER

"True genius resides in the capacity for evaluation of uncertain, hazardous, and conflicting information."

- WINSTON CHURCHILL

Sometimes on projects you are between a rock and a hard place. There seems to be no good solution and your only two choices are bad and worse. Since you are the top leader on the project, everyone is looking at you. Meanwhile the clock continues to tick toward the next milestone and you have to consider that your team may be stuck at an intersection until you tell them which direction to go, wasting time— and time is money (quite literally if you have consultants billing by the hour). We know it's hard, but you have to make a decision, usually without all of the information you'd like and when your back is against the wall. That's just the nature of the role.

In the spirit of sharing lessons from animals, there is a philosophical paradox called *Buridan's Ass*[1] that refers to a hypothetical situation whereby a donkey that is equally hungry and thirsty is placed between a pile of hay and a pail of water and thus cannot decide. Don't suffer the same fate as this poor proverbial animal.

Instead of getting your project stuck in the valley of indecision during its journey, decide who can help provide the information you need to make a decision, and clear your calendar to focus. Be sure that you understand when the decision is needed before it starts to impact the project's performance. Consult your project manager, your boss, other trusted advisors, and/or your steering team if you have one. Listen. Make the best decision you can with the information you have. Be sure your project manager documents it in the decision log, and it is communicated clearly to the right players. And don't worry too much. You can always make another decision later, if more or different information becomes available.

EVIL SPONSOR #3 – THE RISK AVOIDER

Once there was a non-profit leader whose reaction to a basic risk ideation discussion was, "WHY DO YOU HAVE TO BE SO NEGA-TIVE?" Yes, you have to be a positive steward with a can-do attitude. You also have to be realistic. By definition, projects are "unique." As discussed earlier, that means in the history of the world, no one has done quite this same thing, in this time, in this place, with these people...or with other elements that make your project unique. And that means, stuff will happen that no one expects.

Coach your team to go to the project manager with their concerns, because part of the project manager's role is to listen for risks and actively manage them. Let's take another look at #8 from the sponsor's Top 10 Typical Responsibilities, listed earlier in this chapter: *Advise the project manager on anything that is external to the project that might impact its success.* Did you notice that the underlying message here is for you to watch out for risks? It is likely that you are privy to risks that your project team is not. There are inherent risks in paving new roads. Embrace them. Talk about them. Plan to avoid the likely ones. Accept the ones you can't. Be ready for anything. And stand confidently. Your team is watching.

WHAT'S NEXT?

My hope is that this chapter helped you to appreciate the importance and expectations of the *one* project sponsor, the top leader on the project who is represented by the lion. In the next chapter, we'll explore the role of a steering team, and how to decide if you need one.

PRACTICAL PROJECTLAND CHALLENGE

Set your project up for success in the beginning, or reset it if you've already started and aren't sure who the project sponsor is.

Take Action!

1. Identify your ONE project sponsor. If you have more than one candidate for the sponsor role, keep reading to learn about the steering team.

2. Assess how strong your sponsor is. How confident are you in your "lion's" ability to navigate Projectland and perform the top ten responsibilities?

3. No matter how strong the sponsor is, they can't lead this project alone. Consider what you can do to help the sponsor be successful. Take extra time to watch for opportunities to help, particularly if they are new to the role. If you are the sponsor, look at your calendar and determine how you will dedicate the time required to be a positive steward.

4. Define the sponsor role in your version of Projectland. For instance, if you are new to working with your project sponsor, you could share the top ten typical responsibilities in this chapter and use them as an expectation-setting conversation starter. You might say, "Here are the top ten typical responsibilities of the project sponsor. Do you agree this makes sense for our project and in our organization, or do we need to make some adjustments? How can I help?"

5. Download the Top 10 Typical Responsibilities from the Project Guru Press website (projectgurupress.com/meetthe-players/tools) and use it to discuss sponsor role expectations in your organization. If you're the sponsor, keep it nearby as a friendly reminder service.

CHAPTER 6
THE STEERING TEAM IS NOT A COMMITTEE: EAGLES, WHALES, & OWLS, OH MY!

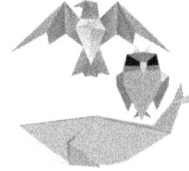

"A committee is a group that keeps minutes and loses hours."
- Milton Berle, Legendary Actor and Comedian

"Dawn. Seriously. This is a LOT of prep for one meeting, and we obviously are supposed to be getting the project done." This was the gripe I heard from one of the team leaders on the biggest, most visible project in the company. The "one meeting" was our first with the project's steering team, which included the griper's boss's boss and all of her peers: the total C-level executive suite, minus the CEO himself. In fact, our project sponsor was the CFO and frequently a guest on MSNBC. We needed to convince him and his peers that we had his $20 million ship with their 100 team members on it under control and not headed for an iceberg. Winging the first meeting would likely be a career-limiting move and result in the equivalent of Lemony Snicket's *A Series of Unfortunate Events* (to reference a popular children's series).

Later, I'll reveal what happened. In the meantime, you might be wondering if your project needs a steering team or not. This is a great question!

DOES MY PROJECT NEED A STEERING TEAM?

Steering teams are created when additional leaders are needed to assist the sponsor in ensuring success of *cross-functional, large, highly visible, complex, risky, or geographically dispersed projects.* While the project in question above had all these characteristics, just one may warrant the creation of a steering team.

Particularly when sponsors don't have 100% control over the impacted resources or expertise in the subject matter of the project, recruiting a steering team is a smart move.

A good rule of thumb to consider is the "80/20 rule." The right sponsor can comfortably make about 80% of the decisions without consulting other leaders. You know you need a steering team when the sponsor needs some help with the other 20%.

Since the chair of the steering team is the sponsor and the clock is always ticking in Projectland, the sponsor ensures that decisions are made in a timely fashion. In fact, final decisions need to be made and fully owned by the sponsor, because ultimately the success of the project lies with the sponsor. To make the best decision possible with the information available at the time, it is wise to consult with the steering team on major decisions and any in which their expertise or perspective could be helpful. Of course, they tend to be busy people and you must respect their time. However, it can be worse not to consult with them on key decisions. Besides, if they signed up to be a steering team member, this is exactly their role, and it's crucial that they share ownership for the trajectory of the project.

For instance, the CFO might be the sponsor of a project to change the way a global company prices its products, because she owns the process and oversees all things financial. Even so, she needs the help of the CIO, because the tech organization is responsible for the new tool that will enable consistent analyses to be performed. She needs the COO on board to ensure that all the salespeople around the world change the way they negotiate deals in the future. She also needs the General Counsel to advise on the impact to customer contracts. Surely in a situation like this, she will be more successful by recruiting these leaders to be part of the project from the beginning.

Again, the chair of the steering team is the sponsor, who is the top boss accountable for the project. As in the example above, you may know that you need the General Counsel because he is ultimately responsible for all customer contracts, and because he is at the right level to help you influence policy changes. But have you considered what other leadership traits he brings to Projectland? Remember, the definition of a project includes that it is unique, which means you are a pioneer in new territory. It can be quite comforting to have experienced leaders as part of your project's leadership team. Good steering team members help you and your project succeed.

WHO ARE THE RIGHT STEERING TEAM MEMBERS? LET'S MEET THESE LEADERS WITH THE HELP OF OUR ANIMAL AVATARS.

As explained in Chapter 4, because the lion can't see the terrain from up above or know what's happening in the sea—and needs wise advice, especially in dark times, to make decisions, steering team members are like *eagles, whales and owls.*

Eagles are great high-level thinkers and well-respected. They see the big picture and keep their eagle eyes focused on the goal. The caution with eagles, is that when they swoop down to grab a detail, they tend to cause utter chaos. But don't worry, once they are satisfied, they go back up to their nest. Also, they are not comfortable and get frustrated when they find themselves in the weeds. They expect you to get straight to the point, and will say things like, "What's the bottom line?"

Whales are leaders with giant responsibilities. When they throw their weight around, they tend to cause major ripples throughout the organization. Whales can dive deep and travel great distances. Beware of when whales are protecting their young, which in Projectland could mean their pet project or their team. Sometimes it helps to remind whales that we need them to think about what is in the best interest of the enterprise, rather than their unit. In organizations, they might lead one of the biggest, most profitable divisions or be viewed as untouchable in some other way. The good news is that when the whale is by your side, you're often protected from predators. Not too many creatures will challenge the whale.

Owls are the wise advisors who have seen it all. When the sponsor is facing a difficult decision or one that requires a savvy political response, the owl will listen and provide sound advice. Owls are known to be nocturnal and wise. Having a leader who thinks differently and is unafraid to persevere when your project is trying to find its way through the darkness, can be a great asset. Don't let their calm demeanor fool you, however. When the owl has a goal, they go after it and can be shrewd.

As I said in Chapter 4, if your project does not need a steering team, GREAT! Life in Projectland is simpler with a single sponsor. Don't force it.

If it does need one to increase your chances of success, also GREAT job figuring it out early before you experience the wrath of miffed executives.

The above descriptions are meant to help you think through what types of perspectives and personalities might be helpful to you, as well as what to watch out for. There are two sides to every coin, so you will get positive leadership attributes right along with the challenging ones. Get ready to up your communication and your "influence without authority" game!

WORDS MATTER – CHANGE YOUR WORDS, CHANGE THE VIBE

We prefer to call this group a TEAM rather than a COMMITTEE to emphasize that we do NOT manage projects by committee. Committees tend to insist on consensus, which leads to meeting after meeting after meeting. I love consensus. I also love McLarens and unicorns, but having one is pretty unrealistic. Acquiring one tomorrow is even more so.

Share the Milton Berle quote at the start of this chapter with the team to emphasize our point! Teams get things done TOGETHER. That's what we need in Projectland. We don't need a committee delaying the project with great debates. Plus, too many cooks in the kitchen make the soup look like sludge and taste like trash.

This is why there must be one head chef, one sponsor, who is ultimately accountable for a timely decision-making process.

WHAT DO STEERING TEAMS DO?

Steering teams steer...as a team. They help the sponsor make sure the project is a success by assisting in timely decision-making and in providing the resources needed per the schedule.

Steering teams are not necessary on every project. However, large, cross-organizational projects are often more successful with a strong and active steering team.

And remember - This is NOT management by committee!

TOP 5 TYPICAL STEERING TEAM RESPONSIBILITIES

1. Support the sponsor with a united front and assist as needed in removing barriers to success
2. Join the sponsor in making critical decisions in a timely fashion
3. Hold the sponsor and team accountable for achieving project objectives and benefits
4. Regularly monitor progress against the plan
5. "Steer" (provide advice and guidance) from both an "enterprise" perspective as well as the perspective of their individual organizations

THE PROFILE OF GOOD STEERING TEAM MEMBERS

Good steering team members are good "enterprise" citizens. This means they are willing to support a decision that is best for the enterprise, even if it is not what they want for their own organization. They are also often strategic thinkers and leaders with influence. They are accessible and provide timely, helpful insights from their experience and perspective. They also are cheerleaders for the team, positive spokespersons, and make the project sponsor aware of any rumblings without being overly dramatic about it. There are always problems to solve, risks to respond to, and issues to resolve. It's just the nature of the place, like heavier traffic during rush hour in a city. The good steering team members embrace that they are in Projectland and operate accordingly. If you have good steering team members, do be sure to sincerely thank them for their support.

BEWARE OF THESE PROJECTLAND VILLAINS

Sadly, evil steering team members do exist. Some of them are excellent at being evil, like Darth Vader from Star Wars, Voldemort from Harry Potter, and The Joker from Batman. None of these characters play well with others, so expecting them to be part of a team, just isn't going to work well. Avoid recruiting them when you can.

Other steering team members aren't trying to be evil. They simply don't realize that their actions are not helping the project stay on track, and are demonstrating undesirable, detrimental Projectland behaviors.

Here are some common evil personas and actions to watch out for. I hope you never have to deal with any of them, but like my mama always says, "Better safe than sorry!"

EVIL STEERING TEAM MEMBER #1 – WING-IT WALLY

These leaders are legitimately busy bees and use this well-known fact to slack off as steering team members. They ignore the seriousness of their advisory role, which is evident when they don't prepare for steering team meetings (e.g., reading the pre-read), and have no idea what you're talking about on a regular basis. Their demeanor is rather unapproachable and they are inaccessible when you need them most. Their approach is to stand on the sidelines rather than getting involved. They may fail to remove obstacles in a timely fashion, even though they promised to take care of something clearly under their control. In summary, they "wing it," spend as little energy as possible on the project, and expect that will be good enough.

EVIL STEERING TEAM MEMBER #2 – THE SNEAKY SABOTEUR

There are several ways steering team members can sabotage the project they are supposed to be helping to lead. Just like snakes slither by nature, some people are just built with undesirable traits for this role.

One version of this reminds me of the ball-hog-athlete fame-monger, who is essentially overshadowing everyone else on the team with "pay attention to me" antics. If we want to give them the benefit of the doubt, we'd say they are confused about the requirement for enterprise thinking. They tend to only worry about their area of responsibility at the potential detriment of what is best for the enter-prise. This shows up on a large project, when one department is jumping up and down screaming they need a feature no one else needs, and holding the whole project's timeline hostage. In the early stages of the project, they may be gentler in their nudging and seem like team players. Then, over time, their tendency to only care about their area sneaks up when they start to become much bolder about it.

This steering team member is quite aptly named the sneaky sabo-teur, sometimes because they are passive aggressive by nature, and other times because they literally want to kill the project or (figura-tively) watch the sponsor go down in flames—or worse, both! They may appear to be supportive during meetings, but work against the team behind the scenes. Beware of the silent type who doesn't speak up. When they see potential collisions or storms coming, particularly those outside the purview of the team, they may decide to do nothing and take the "let them hang themselves" approach.

Sometimes the sabotage is out of jealousy or job-protection. They fear if the project is successful, it might jeopardize their job, either because the results will make them obsolete or because the project itself will expose their weaknesses, and/or make others look more capable. Even though we're all supposed to be on the same team, when people feel fear, they often look out for themselves and don't act like team players at all.

EVIL STEERING TEAM MEMBER #3 - THE GREAT PONTIFICATOR

This steering team member is distracted or overly theoretical. You may wonder what planet they're from because they don't speak Projectland.

They don't listen well, repeating something that was just said five minutes ago with enthusiasm, as if it's their brilliant idea. Or, they speak in hypotheticals or theoretically, rather than offering sound, practical, actionable advice. They believe they have a platform to speak on, and they take every chance they get to jump up on it and hijack meetings with their own agenda. It is impossible to stop by their office quickly because you always end up getting into a long discussion with them about something that generally has no bearing on what you need to keep the project on track. In summary, they not only don't add a lot of practical value to leading the project, but also, they waste time. Since the clock is always ticking in Projectland, it is best to have people who help move things along instead.

THAT'S NOT ALL, FOLKS

Certainly, there are additional evil behaviors that may arise and three that we already covered in the Sponsor chapter. Undesirable leadership traits simply get amplified in Projectland, because most projects that need a steering team are visible, and someone important wishes it was done already.

After reading through the evil personas, you now know why I advise that if your project doesn't meet the profile of needing a Steering Team to help it succeed, then count your lucky stars! If it does, you have an opportunity to up your game, work with leaders in your organization who you may otherwise not meet, and learn a lot!

In Section III, you will learn practical tips for how to recruit the right steering team members who will help your project succeed, and get them on board. And, if you have to work with any of these personas, I'll share stories and tips in the next section to help you identify and deal with these creatures.

🌿

Remember my team member from the start of this chapter, who was lobbying for winging our first steering team meeting with the C-level executives? After it was over, he turned to me and softly said with a quick nod, "I get it now." Then, he strode out of the room with his head held high, because we nailed it. We had a solid story about where we were and why, handled their questions easily, and looked like a confident, cohesive team. While he was still mildly annoyed and would rather have been working on the project (me too!), he never resisted our multiple, intense prep sessions again.

Our C-suite steering team was a great deal of help to us. They made sure that we had the resources we needed to succeed, and since they showed up sharp and prepared, we made sure we were on top of our game for them too. I hope that you also get to work with a great steering team when you need one!

WHAT'S NEXT?

In the next chapter, we'll dive deeper into the person at the center of the Projectland reporting structure: the project manager. (As a refresher, see Chapter 4, Figure 4.1.)

🌿

PRACTICAL PROJECTLAND CHALLENGE

Take Action!

Ask the following questions to determine if you need a steering team.

1. Is your project cross-functional, large, highly visible, complex, risky, or geographically dispersed? If any of these are true, you MAY need a steering team. The more of these attributes that are a YES, the more likely it is that you need one.
2. Will having top leaders on the inside as part of your project's leadership team HELP your sponsor be more successful? Are other leaders who are the sponsor's peers or superiors responsible for a piece of the project, or for the people who will be impacted by the project's product, service or result? The mob movie rule of keeping your friends close and your enemies closer can be rather helpful here!
3. Do you have executives who are STAKEHOLDERS, but who don't really need to be on the inside and help steer? If so, the sponsor and project manager could work with them through the stakeholder management process without forming a steering team.
4. Are you the project manager and do you believe a steering team could help your sponsor? If so, have a conversation ASAP about why you think so, who you think might be helpful, and ask if there is anything you can do to help your sponsor recruit them.
5. The sponsor, as the chair, is the right person to persuade steering team members to be part of this exciting opportunity and help the project be successful. You know you have the right people if the crux of the conversation sounds like, "I really need your help/skills/influence. Without you, this can't be successful, and we shouldn't even start."

If you're a steering team member:

1. Are you clear on your role and responsibilities? If not, you're not alone! Many organizations think steering team members should magically know what to do. Download the Top 5 Role & Responsibilities worksheet from the Project Guru Press website (projectgurupress.com/meettheplayers/tools), have a conversation with your sponsor, and align on expectations.
2. Consider how your organization operates today. Do steering teams operate more like committees where every decision must have consensus? Is this helping or hurting project success? What can you do to influence the organization to a model that is more aligned with the best practices outlined in this chapter?
3. Do you recognize any of the good and evil behaviors in your colleagues or yourself?
4. Review the *Top 5 Typical Steering Team Responsibilities* and objectively assess your performance. What are you doing well? What could you improve? How can you demonstrate what good looks like even more?

CHAPTER 7

THE PROJECT MANAGER: NOT QUITE THE KING (OR QUEEN!) OF THE JUNGLE, BUT AWFULLY CLOSE

> "When the best leader's work is done,
> the people say, 'We did it ourselves.'"
> - Lao Tzu

"**B**ut I don't want to be a project manager. I'm a technical guy. I want to do the technical work. I don't want to do the project management stuff," he said, trying to mask the whine that was totally, absolutely coming through anyway.

I get it. He's not a people person. He chose machines over people for his career. He doesn't see himself as a leader. He just wants to put his head down and do the work he loves and is, frankly, brilliant at doing. So, I asked as gently as possible, "Do you have technical projects that you're fully responsible for, making sure they go well from beginning to end, including the part you do yourself? And are there sometimes things other people have to help you with?"

Long pause. "Yes."

"Then, I'm sorry to have to be the one to break it to you, but in addition to being a technical leader, you're also having to function as a project manager whether you want to admit it or not."

I'm pretty sure I heard a low growl.

Gently, I ask, "Would you like some tips and techniques to make that part easier?"

"Well, yeah…I guess that couldn't hurt," he admits.

"I was a technical person once, too," I said. "I get it. And to be honest, over all these years of being involved in technical projects, I find the people part to be the toughest. Do you?"

"Oh yeah. No doubt," he agrees.

"Ok," I reply. "If you promise to keep an open mind, then I promise to help make the people part easier. Deal?"

"Deal." I think I may have even heard a sigh of relief too.

HOW TO THINK ABOUT THE PROJECT MANAGER ROLE & WHERE IT FITS

No matter the project, the role of a project manager is easy to define but extremely difficult to execute well—whether you consider yourself a people person or not.

Definitions can vary, but a description I like to use in training is that a project manager is *the person responsible for the success of a project, in charge of all aspects of it, and who reports to the sponsor.*

As we discussed earlier, the sponsor is often the person who provides the financial resources, in cash or in kind, for the project, or is the representative of the group who does. The sponsor is like the active owner of a sports team, who provides the funding, sits up in the luxury box visibly showing support, and makes the big decisions.

The project manager is like the head coach on the field who works with the team every day, knows each team member, and helps them become a high performing team that can win together. The relationship between the team owner/sponsor and the head coach/project manager needs to be solid.

WHY THE TIGER IS THE PROJECT MANAGER ANIMAL AVATAR

As discussed earlier, the animal avatar for the sponsor is the lion, because there can really be only one king (or queen!) of the jungle. The animal avatar for the project manager is the tiger. Not quite the lion, but awfully close.

Like the lion, tigers are big, confident cats with strength, skills, smarts, and swagger too. When a tiger wants something, there is little that can stand in its way, as the tiger keeps those incredible eyes focused on the prize. That's just how project managers have to be in the corporate jungle, as well. Like other animals who hunt, tigers benefit from cultivating patience and discerning between when to move and when to wait for the right moment. This savviness is honed over time by both animals and humans, so if you feel like an impatient creature, don't worry! Finally, tigers have stripes and project managers earn their stripes as they manage bigger, hairier, and scarier projects throughout their career. In fact, it can help to remind yourself to harness the elegant power of this incredible cat when you are faced with a difficult situation in Projectland. (Notice I didn't say IF, I said WHEN. It's bound to happen at some point. Because projects are unique by definition, anything can happen and Murphy's Law ("anything that can go wrong will go wrong") is often part of the territory.

TYPICAL PROJECT MANAGER ROLE EXPECTATIONS

What's expected of a project manager in business? Of course, every organization can be a little different. But after working across industries and around the world in Projectland, I've summarized what I believe are the top ten typical responsibilities for project managers.

Project Manager Role:

**Responsible for the success of the project,
in charge of all aspects of it, and report
to the project sponsor.**

TOP 10 TYPICAL PROJECT MANAGER RESPONSIBILITIES

1. Lead the process to define the project and determine how it will be managed
2. Recruit, develop, and lead the team
3. Create the project plan and track progress against that plan, while managing change
4. Provide accurate and timely reporting
5. Make timely decisions and escalate to the sponsor when needed
6. Serve as the single point of contact for all stakeholders, ensuring proper stakeholder management
7. Communicate, communicate, communicate ("90%" of a project manager's job!)
8. "Shield" the team so they can focus on the work
9. Identify, monitor, and respond to issues and risks
10. Lead a smooth transition to operations and close the project properly

As you may have noticed, some responsibilities are important throughout the entirety of the project and others are only required at certain times.

For instance, the first one, "Lead the process to define the project and determine how it will be managed" tends to be a "once and done" task at the beginning of the project.

The fifth one, "Make timely decisions and escalate to the sponsor when needed," happens throughout the entire project. Decision-making is critical at every stage to keep the project moving forward. And of course…number seven, "Communicate, communicate, communicate"—also known as 90% of the job—keeps everyone aligned and rowing in the same direction.

**According to the Project Management Institute:
"Research shows that top project managers spend about 90%
of their time on a project communicating."**

You're a leader now! How you communicate matters and an ability to adapt your style to the situation and audience will make a positive impact. If communication with humans—written and verbal—is not your strength, project management may not be right for you. If you embrace the idea that communication is a skill you want to constantly improve upon, then you're on the right track! Otherwise, if you're forced to manage a project and you're not a communicator, be sure to include someone on your core team who is. Good leaders surround themselves with the talent they lack.

Now, responsibility number ten ("Lead a smooth transition to operations") may seem like it comes at the end of the project, but in order to ensure a smooth transition to operations, you actually need to start engaging operations as early as possible to be sure they'll be ready to take over when the project is complete. Otherwise, they'll throw up their hands, explaining that they don't have the time or resources available. When you haven't involved them appropriately, it feels like you're throwing the project over the fence at them, which simply isn't fair and is downright annoying to both of you. Not involving operations early enough is one of the top root causes we've discovered when organizations complain that their projects take too long to finish.

Remember my analogy that the project manager is like the head coach? Great head coaches are LEADERS who care. And that is what great project managers are, too. This is why I prefer the term *project leader* for this role to emphasize that leadership is what project managers do. The head coach can be awesome or evil just like the other leaders introduced earlier, so if you are the project manager, you get to decide which one you want to be. Besides, the non-leadership functions of project management are ripe for being assumed by artificial intelligence, but that's a story for another book.

PROJECT MANAGERS ARE NOT THESE 3 THINGS

Thing #1[1]. Since project managers are leaders, that means that they are NOT "checklist checker-offers." As one astute leader from a Fortune 100 manufacturer said in an industry report[2], "If you gave me a pilot's checklist, I could probably figure out how to check off all the items. But that doesn't mean I can fly the plane." I promise you that no one wants me trying to fly their plane. And yet, in many organizations, we've seen respected leaders mistakenly think that all you need to do to be a project manager is create a checklist and then make sure everything gets checked off. Oh. So. Wrong. That's like assuming an orchestra conductor just waves his or her arms around to the music.

Sadly, the reason they think this, is because they have encountered people who call themselves project managers, who are running around with a checklist, asking the experts doing the work (sometimes not very politely) if they got a thing on the checklist done. Meanwhile they have no idea what the thing is and won't take "that is not applicable to this project" as an answer. Please, please, please don't do this. It is not only unproductive; it is worse. It gives people the wrong impression about the role, and it sets you up for getting cut in the next round of layoffs. Machines can be checklist checker-offers that don't understand what the thing is either.

Instead of arguing about things they don't understand, the smart project manager works with the experts on their team to develop a plan that makes sense, and a cadence for reporting status on deliverables.

Thing #2. Project managers are NOT stenographers. Stenographers sit silently in the courtroom, expertly taking notes and only speaking when asked to read back the transcript. We already can video record every virtual meeting, which is the ultimate perfect notetaker. Plus, assigning someone to sit silently and taking every word down turns most meeting participants into statues. We need project team members to be creative, speak openly about risks and issues, and be allowed to have fun while they get the work done. We don't want team members to feel nervous that they will be judged. They are not testifying in a court of law, and they may operate as if their lawyers coached them like a witness whose testimony will be on record: to answer as succinctly as possible, keep their emotions in check, and not offer extra information. This is not helpful in Projectland. Rather, we want to encourage team members to speak the truth, the whole truth, and nothing but the truth, and this is much more easily accomplished when people feel safe. It's unfortunate that not everyone speaks the truth at work, and as a leader you need to figure out ways to extract the truth in the most positive way possible.

Since taking good meeting notes in Projectland doesn't mean you take down every word like a stenographer, what do you do? First, don't call them transcripts or meeting minutes. Refer to them as meeting output, meeting summaries, or something else that does not suggest a stenographer-in-the-courtroom situation. Summarizing key decisions and action agreements is more appropriate and recommended.

Thing #3. Project managers are also NOT simply meeting schedulers and coffee fetchers. Interns can schedule meetings. Delivery services can get the coffee. While you may need to do these things, remember that you are a leader who adds value, keeps the project moving in the right direction, and creates a healthy culture that gets results. In summary, do not let administrivia be the only things people see you doing, or people will think that you are an administrative assistant who deserves the assistant's pay grade. Unfortunately, the administrator's compensation doesn't often reflect all the value that they provide to keep the organization humming. I know this, because my mother was in this role, and she worked SO HARD doing all kinds of things that needed to be done and no one else would do, including project management when necessary.

A Special Note for Administrative Professionals!
If you are an administrator today, I encourage you to consider whether

project management is a fit for your next formal role. Talented admin-
istrators who have attended my practical project management classes
have had lightbulbs go off for them that say, "I can totally do this and
get paid a lot more!" Or, "Thank you for all the tips to help me with
the projects on my plate, as well as the clarity about the role. I'd like to
stay just where I am." Both responses are a win in my book. (Oh wait.
This IS my book.) Either way, don't be surprised if your superpowers
around communicating and organizing land you an important project
to manage.

Now that we've covered three of the things project managers are
NOT, let's talk about what smart project managers SHOULD do to
avoid these common misperceptions. Let's consider timeless advice
from Sun Tzu's *The Art of War*[3]: "Know the enemy, know yourself;
your victory will never be endangered. Know the ground, know the
weather; your victory will then be total."

Since that quote is chock full of information, let's dive deeper into
each component:

Know the Enemy – Do your research. Be clear on what you're up
against in achieving your project's objectives. This could be external
competition or internal potential saboteurs who are threatened by your
success and want you to fail. It could be that the technology you need
to implement is brand new and full of bugs. Or the culture is "no, slow,
and status quo," as a government client just shared with me. Some
organizational cultures are indeed the enemy of progress and
achieving results.

Know Yourself. Know your strengths and weaknesses. Plan
accordingly. For instance, if you are great at the big picture and terrible
at the details, you'll need good team leads. If you're new to project
management, get a seasoned coach. If you're not sure how you're
going to get the humans ready for the change your project brings,
include an expert change management pro on your team.

Know the Ground. This is your version of Projectland. Do you
know the rules for how to get stuff done in your organization? Is it
going to be a steep climb for your team to get to the top of the mountain? Will it be easier or harder to come back down and cross the finish

line? What kinds of creatures might pop out from behind a rock and scare you off your planned trail? What skills and equipment are you going to need to give your team the best shot at winning?

Know the Weather. This is the environment. This could mean market forces, the economy, the political climate, and the seasons inside your organization. Seasons could mean budget season, closing the books season when all the finance folks need to focus, conference season, and holiday season. All must be considered as you plan.

It is said that when Napoleon invaded Russia, he was defeated by "General Winter" (referring to the unusually brutal weather). Is there an equivalent of "General Winter" in your organization? If so, work with your team to plan accordingly. When I traveled through Scotland at the end of March, I experienced all of the seasons in a single day. The cute, flat boots that were perfect for working in London and week-ending in Edinburgh weren't cutting it in the Highlands. Since I like the outdoors and wanted to walk everywhere, snow boots I could hike in were just what the Scottish ski shop owner prescribed. And they made all the difference. So, if you don't know exactly how to manage your project through your organization's environment safely, ask someone who does.

A WORD ABOUT AGILE PROJECTS

Have you heard any of these words flying around your organization: terms *Agile, Scrum, Kanban, Extreme Programming (XP), Test-Driven Development (TDD)?* Since the Agile Manifesto was born in Utah in 2001 by a global group of software developers rebelling against the waterfall establishment in search of a better way, Agile has piqued the interest of businesses who want to deliver better working code faster. When I first started to learn about these methods, because a project leader just can't have enough project tools in her toolbox, I realized that I was already doing a lot of this, because to me, it was common sense. Later I had the opportunity to teach Agile for Teams, Scrum, Scrum Masters, and Product Owners inside major tech companies, which was a lot of fun. Plus, there have been many instances since then where I was able to suggest to non-tech project teams, "What if we took a page out of the Agile playbook and tried this?"

What is *Agile?* Agile is a framework with a set of principles that is like an umbrella encompassing all of those other "flavors" I mentioned above. Notice I avoided the words method and methodology, which are no-no's to utter in the presence of Agile purists. Also note the year the manifesto was born. *Agile. Is. Not. New.*

Here are some things I like about it and have employed successfully on even non-tech projects in non-agile environments to help the project team reach its goals efficiently.

- Set up the team to create the deliverables in iterations in close collaboration with the customer.
- Prioritize what the team will focus on with the customer, sponsor, or small group of key leaders.
- Define time periods for the team to present its work to key stakeholders and get friendly feedback. Set expectations that the presentation of the work is not meant to be perfect. It's meant to show progress.
- Welcome and expect change, and accommodate change requests as part of the iterative creating and refining process.
- Emphasize teamwork, transparency, a smart cadence, and implementing lessons learned (also known as a *retrospective* in Scrum) to make the experience better for everyone every time.

What does this mean for you as a project manager? It all starts with number 1 on our Top 10 Typical Project Manager Responsibilities list: *Lead the process to define the project and determine how it will be managed.* Agile is a tool in the project manager's toolbox. It is a useful approach when the culture enables close collaboration between team members and the customer, and when "figuring it out together" via iterative change is an acceptable part of the process. It would NOT, for example, be a recommended approach to try during the construction phase of a bridge or facility.

Many organizations have tried agile and failed. When this happens it is often because culture doesn't support the collaborative Agile principles and/or because they try to create their own cherry-picked hybrid approach and then blame agile when it doesn't work.

In any case, all of the Top 10 Typical Project Manager Responsibilities still apply. Even when teams claim to be "self-led", everyone has a boss and stakeholders with expectations. *Someone* needs to:

- Staff the team and address team concerns
- Keep senior management apprised (Managers always want to know "What are we getting for the money, and when?")
- Escalate issues to the sponsor as needed (Even in an Agile project, *someone* is paying for it and authorized it!)
- Manage change (Even though Agile projects expect and are great at managing change, they DON'T expect oscillation! Change and corresponding expectations must be carefully managed.)
- Communicate with stakeholders and ensure proper stakeholder management
- Manage issues and risks, and shield the team from outside interference

If you're the project manager, this someone is *you*.

CONCLUSION

The top ten typical responsibilities of a good project manager operating as an empowered leader may seem daunting, and it is. Great project leaders are constantly assessing and evaluating the project to ensure these tremendous responsibilities are met regularly. They're always thinking, communicating, listening for issues and risks, ensuring tasks are completed, and focusing on how to help the team meet the project goals. In other words, the project manager's job is to do whatever they need to do to help the team do what THEY need to do when they need to do it.

If you are in the role of project manager, and serious about being the best project manager you can be, then take a deep breath and square your shoulders. It's time for you to step up and lead your team through Projectland. Being a good project manager can often feel like the Wizard of Oz, behind the curtain, pulling the levers, turning the gears, and working harder than anyone realizes. And in the end, helping the team be successful at delivering the product, service, or result as promised, can be so very satisfying.

WHAT'S NEXT?

Now that we've learned about the sponsor, steering team, and project manager roles, let's talk teamwork. With the help of three animal avatars, we'll introduce different characteristics to consider so that you can evaluate whether you feel you have the right team members to help you meet your project objectives (or not!). We'll discuss what great team members do differently and the top ten responsibilities of a team member in Projectland. Additionally, we'll discuss the role of Team Lead, when this role can be extremely helpful, and what is often expected of them. Teamwork really does make the dream work in Projectland.

PRACTICAL PROJECTLAND CHALLENGE

What will *you* do with what you've learned?

1. Review the Project Manager Top 10 Responsibilities

- Are these reflective of the responsibilities of project managers where you work?
- If you're in the project manager role, in which responsibilities do you feel confident? In which do you feel challenged?
- If you are working with a project manager, in which responsibilities do you feel they are strong? In which do you

feel they are challenged? How can you help them succeed?

2. Think about whether it makes sense for the project sponsor and project manager to discuss and accept or revise their respective top ten responsibility lists. Get the role and responsibility handouts at the Project Guru Press website (projectgurupress.com/meettheplayers/tools) and plan for a positive conversation about expectations. For example, are all ten of these expected for each role? Do you both agree with the lists? Is there anything missing?

3. It's best not to assume that you can read minds. Plan to update the responsibility lists according to your conversation and what makes sense in your organization. Clearly defining the sponsor and project manager roles, and knowing what is expected, will set both of these critical leaders up for a successful working relationship!

CHAPTER 8
THE DREAM TEAM: THE FAST, THE STRONG, & THE FURIOUSLY FUN

"Teamwork makes the dream work,
but a vision becomes a nightmare when the
leader has a big dream and a bad team."
- John C. Maxwell, Leadership Expert & Bestselling Author[1]

According to an article on Olympics.com[2], possibly the greatest team ever assembled in sports was the USA men's basketball team at the 1992 Barcelona Olympics, commonly known as "The Dream Team."

The team had Magic – literally. Earvin 'Magic' Johnson, Michael Jordan, and Larry Bird, three of the greatest players of all time, along with David Robinson, Patrick Ewing, Karl Malone, Charles Barkley, John Stockton, Scottie Pippen, Clyde Drexler, and Chris Mullin. Christian Laettner was the only member of the team without NBA experience.

The Dream Team was formed after the governing body for international basketball voted overwhelmingly to allow professional basketball players to compete in the Olympics, as was the case for soccer, ice hockey, and tennis.

What was surprising to me is that the USA voted against the proposal.[3] That said, the rule change made sense. Many of the international players to date had been men who became NBA players, and the US players were largely college students who played an entirely different game. The world had become more global, and it was time to reflect that in the rules.

Fortunately, The Dream Team did live up to its name. Did you know that Jordan was NOT the highest scorer? That accolade went to Charles Barkley with 18 points per game vs. Jordan's 14.9. However, Jordan did set the record for most assists in a single Olympic game (12). Now that's proof of a great team player!

The Dream Team also did more than decisively win the Olympic Gold. Johnson said, "It had such a big global impact on the game, and it allowed kids around the world to dream that they can play in the NBA one day. The game grew in popularity, and it grew in terms of our own personal brands...I mean Michael Jordan became even bigger."

Teamwork makes the dream work, they say. With twelve superstars on that first pro basketball team allowed in the Olympics, it could have gone very differently. Had they not formed as a team, respected one another, and acted like professionals on and off the court, the Olympics could have chosen to reverse its decision or at least regretted it mightily.

DRAWING PROJECTLAND LESSONS FROM THE DREAM TEAM

What parallels can you draw from The Dream Team in your world? I found three.

First, it is not unusual for teams in business to deliver additional goals or benefits beyond the obvious "create product, service, or results" objectives. For instance, I've seen and suggested that turning around the reputation of the organization responsible for delivering the project can be an unwritten and very real objective. When that has been the case, and the right people have been assigned with the right attitudes, this strategy has worked well! Additionally, successful project people have raised their own personal reputations in their workplaces and industries too. What other unspoken project objectives might there be for you?

Second, in reflecting on how The Dream Team could have become an ego-fueled nightmare, we're reminded how the lack of teamwork, not having the right skills available at the right time to get the job done, or infecting the team with negative attitudes is the stuff of Projectland nightmares too. In my career, when egos, self-serving behavior, or negative attitudes are involved, the project experience can be downright disastrous. When people respect each other for what they bring to the table, including differing opinions, even the most challenging projects can become a career highlight! When you have smart people who work together well and want to do the right thing, you can do anything! Which type of project team do you have?

Lastly, The Dream Team was formed in response to a rule change, and many projects and therefore project teams have been formed by rule changes too! For example, the euro[4] was introduced on January 1, 1999, first as an 'invisible currency' used only for accounting and electronic payments, and then on January 1, 2002, when physical coins and banknotes were born. The result? Across 12 EU countries, the biggest cash changeover in history took place. This forced every entity operating globally to launch projects, and more importantly, required cross-functional, international teams to work together to deliver these projects—people who may not have had to work together in the past.

Another example is when the government sets standards that organizations need to meet. For instance, The Clean Air Act (CAA)[5] is a comprehensive federal law in the United States that regulates air emissions from stationary and mobile sources. When the Act was amended in 1990[6] to set new goals (dates) for achieving National Ambient Air Quality Standards (NAAQS), many corporations needed to launch projects to comply, and approximately 25,000 dry cleaners started shaking in their boots[7]. Again, cross-functional teams needed to be formed to address the standards changes on time. While we'll explore more about cross-functional teams a little later in the chapter, what about your world? Are there any projects that have been formed in response to a rule change, thus requiring new, cross-functional teams to meet the challenge?

Now that you've had the chance to think about The Dream Team, one of the most successful and famous teams in sports, along with parallels in your world, let's dive deeper into what makes a great team in Projectland.

MEET OUR PROJECTLAND ANIMAL AVATAR DREAM TEAM

To help you plan for the right team makeup that will help your project be a success, and maybe, possibly, even make the experience a little fun, let's meet our next three animal avatars. These beautiful creatures are all great team players in the animal kingdom with special skills: *gazelles, bison, and dolphins.*

Gazelles are fast. Did you know that the gazelle can outrun a cheetah by dodging and weaving and getting the cheetah to break its stride? Gazelles remind us that in Projectland the clock is always ticking. Sponsors always seem to want us to deliver faster. Plus, drawing a straight line between where you are today and where you want to go, is the best way to achieve your goal in theory, but not always in reality. You need someone on your team who can move fast even when there are risks and the environment is stressful. Especially when your project has an intense schedule, you need someone who is like a gazelle to help you deliver faster because of their skills, approach to getting work done, or both.

Arianna Huffington reveals in her #1 New York Times bestselling book, *Thrive*,[8] that her screensaver is a picture of gazelles. "They are my role models," she says. "They run and flee when there is danger—a leopard or a lion approaching—but as soon as the danger passes, they stop and go back to grazing peacefully without a care in the world." She goes on to suggest, "We need to liberate ourselves from the tyranny of our fight-or-flight mechanism. And yet much of our life has actually been structured so that we live in an almost permanent state of fight-or-flight—here comes another dozen emails calling out for a response; must stay up late to finish the project; I'll just use these four minutes of downtime to return six more calls." Oh how wonderful it is to have a gazelle on the team to model the behavior of being able to move fast when necessary, and also calmly do what needs doing!

Bison are strong. They remind us that we need to focus on people's strengths and recruit people for their strengths. Plus, bison team members aren't afraid to stand firm on an issue even in the face of adversity. Since projects are unique by definition, there are always problems to solve in Projectland. Did you know that bison will turn into a snowstorm because walking into the storm will get them out of the weather quicker?[9] Having a strong team member who is not only unafraid of the storm, but whose inclination is to walk right into it can be phenomenally helpful. Did you know that bison are also fast? They can run up to 35 miles per hour. In addition, they're extremely agile, which is especially impressive considering they can weigh up to 2,000 pounds. Bison can spin around quickly, jump high fences and are strong swimmers[10]. If you can, choose a team member like the bison— someone who knows their stuff, is a strong team player, and can help the team move fast too. In other words, someone who's like a Swiss Army knife, because the smaller the team, the easier it is to manage. This versatile person has the fortitude to push through a problem and drive results even when the going gets tough. Ain't nobody stoppin' a bison!

According to the Disney Institute, an ideal team should be a mix of both results-oriented and relationship-oriented people. If your project is highly technical, I'll make the case later for why this mix can be an even more important contributor to success than most people think! The gazelle and the bison are largely focused on results. Our final avatar makes sure the relationship part isn't forgotten: the dolphin.

Dolphins are fun. Our third and final dream team avatar is from the sea. You may have heard that dolphins swim and hunt together in groups, called pods. They are smart, social creatures who love to play and have their own language. They make a variety of sounds, including whistles, clicks, squawks, squeaks, moans, barks, groans, and yelps. They are also fast sprinters. Bottlenose dolphins can even reach speeds of over 30 miles per hour for brief periods![11] The dolphin reminds us that communication is important both inside and outside the team. For example, on projects where the objective is to change the way people do their work, like automating a paper process or replacing a software system, you're going to need someone who can prepare people for the change, train them on how to do their work, and communicate what they need to know when they need to know it. Dolphins also remind us that even though Projectland is intense, it's important for the team to have a little fun while we dive together into unknown territory.

PROJECT TEAMS ARE OFTEN CROSS-FUNCTIONAL

In addition to needing team members with different work styles and strengths, many projects need to recruit team members from different functional groups (e.g., finance, human resources, and technology) or with a specific skillset (e.g., cost accounting, payroll, and artificial intelligence). This is why some organizations refer to team members as "Subject Matter Experts" or SMEs. Even if team members don't self-identify as experts in the beginning of the project, they surely will be by the end! No one else in the organization will know as much as they do about the part of the product, service, or result that they helped to deliver. No one. In addition, cross-functional teams expose you to new areas of the organization and create an opportunity for you to build relationships with people you may not otherwise meet. These are just some of the reasons why projects can be a great career opportunity!

Project Team Member Role:

A project team consists of subject matter experts responsible for completing deliverables, "planning the work and working the plan.[12]"

Team members report to project team leads, if that role exists, or directly to the project manager.

It is best when team members exit their day jobs and enter Projectland where they report to the team lead, if that role exists, or directly to the project manager. Before we talk about team leads, let's explore the top ten typical responsibilities of all team members.

TOP 10 TYPICAL TEAM MEMBER RESPONSIBILITIES

1. Understand project objectives, your contribution, and have your elevator speech ready
2. Accurately estimate the work and report progress
3. Make the project manager aware of issues and risks that may impact accomplishing agreed-upon activities or the overall objectives of the project
4. Ensure team member availability is included in the project schedule before the baseline is finalized
5. Direct change requests to the project manager no matter how minor they may seem
6. Especially when on the critical path[13], keep commitments (or the entire project will be impacted)
7. Employ a positive, problem-solving attitude. Trust that the "problem of the day" will be resolved by tomorrow.
8. Communicate status carefully outside of the team
9. Recognize that teaming is a process. (This is the subject of "Chapter 12: Get Ready for the Storm: Teaming is a Process, Too.")
10. Be the best team member you can be. Employ patience, respect, and help your teammates.

Let's dive deeper into a few of the responsibilities that tend to trip up team members who are new to Projectland. Please note that I'll be speaking directly to team members with these tips. If you are part of the project leadership team, keep reading! You need to understand how to support team members in Projectland, and these tips will help you do just that.

TIP 1: GET INSPIRED BY THE BIG PICTURE

As you may have noticed, some responsibilities are important throughout the project and others are required at certain times.

For instance, the first one, "Understand project objectives, your contribution, and have your elevator speech ready," is critical in the beginning or when you're first joining the team. Don't make the mistake of just understanding what you're being asked to do. Seek to understand the overall objectives of the project, why it's important to the big picture, and how you fit.

In Angela Duckworth's book, *Grit: The Power of Passion and Perseverance*[14], she recaps the story of the bricklayers. Three bricklayers are asked: "What are you doing?" The first says, "I am laying bricks." The second says, "I am building a church." And the third says, "I am building the house of God."

Not only does the third bricklayer understand the big picture, but also he goes about his work with an entirely different attitude than the others. He understands and connects with it on a different, much more inspiring level.

There is a similar story about how King Arthur called for stone-cutters to build Camelot. Two stonecutters were told only to make stones. One provided small rocks, the other provided giant boulders. They recruited a third stonecutter and clarified that it was to build a castle in Camelot. Finally, they got the right kind of stones, because the vision was made clear to the team members responsible for doing the work. This is why it is so important for project leaders to take the time to explain the project vision, and for team members to ask questions until they feel confident that they understand it.

When you understand the WHY behind the project and the big picture, you can also feel more connected, inspired, and motivated to do a great job and be a great team player. As illustrated by the stone-cutters, you can also contribute better, and ensure your efforts will be fruitful. Note that the bricklayers' answers are also their elevator speeches. Be sure you have a good answer ready when someone stops and asks what you're doing.

TIP 2: ACCURATE ESTIMATES – HAHAHAHAHAHA!

Earlier we mentioned that "accurate estimate" is an oxymoron. It's an estimate. Synonyms of estimate include *approximation, guess,* and *ballpark figure.* It often feels like you're getting out your crystal ball and predicting the future.

Team members are often asked to estimate how long a deliverable will take to complete. Then the project manager strings all those estimates together to answer the question everyone wants to know, which is, "When will the project be done?"

Consider a team with ten SMEs that basically have to work like they're running a relay race. As soon as one person is done, they hand their piece to the next person to continue, and so on and so forth, until they get to the end of the race.

Now imagine each SME says their leg of the race will take two weeks to run. The project would be done in twenty weeks (two weeks each for ten people). For the sake of keeping the example simple, we'll exclude project closure activities, which might take another two weeks.

This is the wrong way to estimate in Projectland. Why?

What if each team member had estimated two weeks simply because they were scared of being wrong or getting distracted by other work? This happens all the time with team members. They pad their estimates "just in case." In this example, what if they really felt that if they were locked in their favorite room with their favorite music and favorite food delivered under the door, it would probably only take them one day each? In that case, the project team's part would just take ten days—or two business weeks. See the problem? Two weeks vs. twenty weeks, and we're talking about only a ten-person team.

If you're a team member being asked for estimates, simply do your best. Don't expect they will be accurate, particularly if you've never done this thing before in this environment. Explain your reasoning, your worries (these are risks), and perhaps consider your optimistic, realistic, and pessimistic estimates. Meaning, if everything goes well, the weather is great and you're having a good day, you might run a one-mile race in seven minutes. If conditions were poor and you forgot your running shoes, you might have to walk instead, and the same mile would take you fourteen minutes. Realistically, you may feel nine minutes is a fair estimate of your abilities overall. If it helps you feel better about the estimate you're submitting, plan to talk this logic through with your team lead or project manager.

If you're nervous about providing your estimate or you want to get a little fancy, check out the practical pro-tip about how to leverage the PERT technique available on the Project Guru Press website (projectgurupress.com/meettheplayers/tools).

Now let's build on our example. That's because, in addition to the team members estimating individual tasks, some project managers then add an overall project contingency on top of everyone's estimates, which is fine, and in most cases recommended. Usually this is a minimum of 10%. So if all ten team members had submitted their inflated two-week estimates with their own contingency (for a total of twenty weeks), and then, if the project manager adds the 10% contingency on top of that, the total comes to twenty-two weeks (again, not including project closure).

Compare that to 10% of the more accurate ten-day estimate, which is one day, for a total of eleven days. Clearly, the difference between twenty-two weeks (nearly six months!) and eleven days (less than two weeks) is enormous. If you're researching a custom product online that you really want, and you see an option to have it created and delivered in eleven days vs. twenty-two weeks, with all else being equal (price, reviews, etc.), I'm not a gambling woman, but I bet 99% of humans would select the eleven-day option.

Timing of estimates are important to consider, too. Early on in a project, a project manager is often asked to provide a rough or "order-of-magnitude" estimate. Or, the project sponsor may offer a gut feel that the project can be delivered in "six months" or "by the end of the year." Unfortunately, SMEs are often not consulted at this early stage when the project is really just an idea, because they haven't been assigned to the project yet. Later, after the project is approved, team members are assigned, the work is defined, more reasonable estimates are gathered, and the project manager can lead the work to develop the full project schedule and budget. The Project Management Institute refers to this as *progressive elaboration*. In other words, the more that is known about the project, the more accurate the estimates will become. This is why providing accurate updates on your progress is so important throughout the project. In essence, you are always providing a more accurate estimate about what has been done, and what is left to do.

One more thing that will hopefully help you feel better is that projects are often like a relay race. Your contribution may not be needed until later, in which case you'll get that two-week warning so that you can find your special room, stock it with your favorite snacks, and hang a sign on the door that says, "Important project deliverables under construction. Do not disturb."

TIP 3: THE CRITICAL PATH IS INDEED CRITICAL

Now you also need to know what the sixth responsibility means: *Especially when on the critical path, keep your commitments (or the entire project will be impacted).*

The relay race is a great illustration for the critical path concept. If you estimated that your leg of the race takes seven minutes, and you forget your running shoes and take fourteen minutes, then the remaining team members who are next in the lineup will be impacted. They'll have to try to make up the time to finish the race and win. The closer your piece is to the end, the harder that is to do. This is again why we also need you to accurately report progress, which is suggested in the second responsibility.

If you run into something unexpected, the project manager will have to figure out another path to victory. Communicate the issue as soon as possible, to give your team the best shot at delivering on schedule. Don't go it alone! That's why you have a team. It's very possible that another team member may be able to help you. For instance, maybe they have a pair of new shoes for you to borrow, or they can run your part while you get your shoes, and then you can run their part instead. This is an example of why working as a team to overcome challenges can be so beneficial in Projectland.

TIP 4: BEWARE OF DIRECT CHANGE REQUESTS

When a stakeholder comes to you directly and says something like, "Can you just do this one little thing, please? I'm sure it will only take you five minutes," you need to harness your inner Nancy Reagan and "just say NO."[15]

But since you're a nice person and you agree it will only take you five minutes; you want to say yes. Resist the temptation and do not set a precedent that you are a pushover. The next request may take much longer. Plus, the thing that only takes you five minutes to change may have much greater downstream impacts. This is why responsibility number five is: *Direct change requests to the project manager no matter how minor they may seem.*

There have been so many times when overly accommodating, unsuspecting team members embraced the Nike slogan and just did it, and did not realize that the five-minute change on their particular gear jammed up the whole system. Your best response to any change request could simply be, "I'd love to help you. Let's check-in with the project manager first."

Now that we've covered some key concepts, tips, and pitfalls for team members, let's talk about the role of the team lead.

TEAM LEADS ARE LIKE THE ALPHA ANIMALS

As introduced in "Chapter 4: Who's Who in Projectland," the Team Lead is a typical role needed for geographically dispersed, technically complex, or larger projects. Team leads are often subject matter experts who coordinate the work of fellow experts to plan and create project deliverables. Just like there are a few elder, alpha animals in a herd, team leads tend to be respected and experienced leaders in their areas of expertise.

Great team leads embrace the top ten typical responsibilities above, help team members do the same, and lead by example.

"The best example of leadership is leadership by example."

- JERRY MCCLAIN

TEAM LEADS REPORT TO THE PROJECT MANAGER

In Projectland, team leads report to the project manager. If you have been assigned as a team leader, this means that you and the project manager need to create a cooperative relationship. Do not expect the project manager to know your field of expertise or culture of the organization. If they did, they probably wouldn't need you on the project. Help your project manager understand what they need to know to support your team in a positive way.

When the project manager asks questions, they are often not questioning YOU. Good project managers ask questions to understand how to help you and your crew be successful in delivering your portion of the product, service, or result on time, on budget, on scope, on quality, and with a high degree of stakeholder satisfaction. They are also responsible for understanding how your portion of the project puzzle fits with the other pieces, so that in the end, all of the pieces create the vision of the future that the project promised.

TEAM LEADS & PROJECT MANAGERS NEED A POSITIVE PARTNERSHIP

Good team leads develop an open, honest, and respectful relationship with their project manager. Some team leads seem to operate as if the project manager should be on a "need to know basis," are not accurate in how they report progress, and take a defensive posture when the project manager asks questions. These behaviors create a toxic environment that can degrade the team's results and discourage them.

Project managers and team leads need to work together to create a healthy environment that gets results; exhibiting a positive partnership goes a long way to ensuring that all the creatures in Projectland feel safe and supported. These are leadership roles, and the team is watching what they do and how they work. They are listening to the team leads' and project manager's words and tone. They want to trust and feel confident in their ability to lead them through the unknown, terrifying territory of Projectland. To operate at their best, they need to see that they are allies, not adversaries.

WHAT'S NEXT?

Congratulations! You've now learned about all of the roles on the project team: the lion leader; the whale, eagle and owl steering team members; the tiger project manager; and the gazelle, bison, and dolphin team leads and talented team members. Next, let's meet our final set of players in Projectland. It's time to explore the wild world of stakeholders.

PRACTICAL PROJECTLAND CHALLENGE

Here are some ideas for what you can do with what you've learned.
    Take Action!

1. Consider your work culture. Are there parallels you can draw from the USA men's basketball team at the 1992 Barcelona Olympics, also known as The Dream Team, to help you influence the right project culture?

2. Consider your project team. What creatures do you see in your version of Projectland?

- For more analysis about the helpful and potentially hurtful characteristics all of the animal avatars bring to the table, check out "Appendix D: Animal Avatar Analyses."
- If you're not feeling like your team members embody the characteristics of the gazelle, bison, or dolphin, or just want to check out additional animal avatar options, check out "Appendix E: Additional Animal Avatars in the Projectland Zoo."

3. Consider the Projectland Dream Team Animal Avatars:

- Who's who in your version of Projectland?

- How can you best leverage their natural abilities to make the project a great career experience and your project more successful?
- Do you have people who are team players, and a balance of results-oriented and relationship-oriented people?
- How many people are in stretch roles vs. actual experts?
- Do you have the right people in the right roles with the experience, expertise, and characteristics that you need?

4. Review the Top 10 Typical Team Member Responsibilities:

- Are these reflective of the responsibilities of project team members where you work?
- If you're a team member on a project, in which responsibilities do you feel confident? In which do you feel challenged?
- If you are a team member working with a project manager or team lead, how can you create a positive partnership with them? How can you help them in their roles?
- If you are a project manager or team lead with team members reporting to you on the project, how can you help them succeed?

5. Think about whether it makes sense to discuss and accept or revise the top 10. Get the role and responsibility handouts at the Project Guru Press website (projectgurupress.com/meettheplayers/tools) and plan for a positive conversation about expectations. For example, are all 10 of these responsibilities expected for all team members? Is there anything missing?

6. It's best not to assume that you or your team can read minds. Plan to update the responsibility lists according to your conversation and what makes sense in your organization. Clearly defining the expectations of the team members and team leads will set them and the project up for success!

CHAPTER 9

THREE SURPRISING KINDS OF STAKEHOLDERS

> "You can please some of the people all of the time,
> you can please all of the people some of the time,
> but you can't please all of the people all of the time."
> — John Lydgate, Poet[1]

W hen I started managing projects, I'm not sure anyone introduced me to the concept of stakeholders. Over the years, I've learned that these people can make or break your project. In fact, the chapter opening quote above is great advice to heed in your planning. Since you cannot please all of the people all of the time, project leaders need to figure out which stakeholders are most important, create a plan, and ensure action is taken. More on how to do that later. First, let's explore who stakeholders are and why they're so important to consider.

For instance, let's say you're planning to throw a Funday Sunday wicked fraternity house style party, with a live band and outdoor lawn games, where the end time is based on whoever can stay upright the longest. WOOHOO! If your party gets too loud and obnoxious, your uptight neighbors could, and probably will, call the police. The annoyed neighbors are stakeholders. They are outside your house and weren't invited inside to party. If they are inconvenienced, annoyed or even perceive that they could be impacted in any way by your party, they could cause problems for you. And frankly, you should see this situation coming. With a little planning, you can figure out how to party and avoid police interference.

In this chapter, we'll cover practical tips, animal avatars, and typical stakeholders you'll likely need to consider, so that you can begin to navigate the human side of delivering any project successfully.

MORE ON WHO PROJECT STAKEHOLDERS ARE & WHO THEY ARE NOT

So far, we've covered the players on the project team, including the subject matter experts and project leaders such as the sponsor, steering team, project manager, and team leads.

Everyone else who cares about the project is considered a *stakeholder*.

Remember the question from Chapter 4? Doesn't the team have a stake in the project too? Absolutely! But again, to keep it simple, we refer to the people who are *outside* of the project team as stakeholders.

Let's also recall the Project Management Institute definition of a stakeholder as "an individual, group, or organization that may affect, be affected by, or perceive itself to be affected by a decision, activity, or outcome of a project, program, or portfolio." Since it's such a mouthful, this rhyming version of my translation will hopefully make it easier to remember:

Stakeholders are people outside your team...

...who love your project, hate your project, or are somewhere in between.

You might also be wondering: *What's the difference between a resource and a stakeholder?* Generally, I call the human resources that are working on the project "team members." To keep it simple, we refer to a "resource" or "team member" as anyone you would assign a task to complete on the project schedule, and a "stakeholder" as anyone else who's outside of the project team (and may love or hate your project or be somewhere in between these extremes).

STAKEHOLDER SATISFACTION IS PROBABLY MORE IMPORTANT THAN YOU THINK

No one disputes whether or not a project is successful when the product, service, or result is delivered on time, on budget, on scope, on quality, and with a high degree of stakeholder satisfaction. Unfortunately, and as evidenced by the terrible statistics introduced at the beginning of our journey, achieving all five of these delivery objectives is really, really, REALLY hard to do.

Even if you are able to deliver on time, on scope, on cost, and on quality, will you automatically achieve a high degree of stakeholder satisfaction?

Well….that depends. It's hard to satisfy everyone and some people are never satisfied.

For instance, I read the star ratings on Amazon recently for a product I was considering buying. It had a lot of five-star reviews. It also had some one-star reviews. It was like reading a one-star review for a standard washing machine that says, "It washes the clothes okay, but the clothes come out wet. They aren't dry. One star for you!" Don't be surprised if you, too, encounter project stakeholders who are out to lunch, hopeless, or interested in tarnishing your five-star reputation.

I used to think that delivering results were all that mattered, but now I know differently. If you think back to our epic frat-house-style party, this concept becomes clear. When the police shut down our party and guests run screaming into the night, and some of them get caught and have to spend the night in jail, it doesn't matter if the party was great up until that point. All they will remember is having to beg for bail money.

Later, I'll introduce practical tips and a thinking tool to help you navigate the human side of delivering any project successfully. For now, let's explore the three different categories of stakeholders to get your mental gears turning, and our corresponding animal avatars to help make it a little more fun.

WHAT ARE THE THREE SURPRISING KINDS OF STAKEHOLDERS?

Okay, I realize if you've read the "Who's Who in Projectland" chapter, the answer may not exactly be a surprise anymore. But as mentioned earlier, it can be helpful to categorize stakeholders into three groups:

1. Cheerleaders – the people who love your project
2. Saboteurs – the people who hate your project
3. Finicky fans – the people who are somewhere in between

Let's explore each of the three categories a bit further and re-introduce our animal avatars to make it a little less boring.

Cheerleaders: These are the people who are SO EXCITED about your project. The animal avatar for these stakeholders is the *happy dog*. I hate leaving my dog, Lita, at home alone, but when I come back, even after a short time, she goes wild with excitement. The key with the cheerleaders is to keep them engaged and to focus their excitement on taking positive action so they don't accidentally get in the way. For example, when my fifty-pound furball gets underfoot when I'm cooking, it's because she knows I'm a messy cooker and will invariably drop something on the floor that she might like to clean up. I'm sure she thinks she's being helpful, but I could trip over her if I'm not paying attention.

Saboteurs: These folks are NOT supportive of your project. They may feel threatened by it or by you and actively work against you. I've been on projects where people were worried that the project was going to result in their or their colleagues' jobs being changed or cut completely. And then there's the fact that most people REALLY don't like change. And guess what projects usually do...bring change. The animal avatar for the saboteur stakeholder is the *snake*. If you don't realize there's a snake in the grass and you step near it, it will bite you. Snakes can infect your project with negativity and even get it canceled.

Finicky Fans: I spent 20 years in Philadelphia, where sports fans are well known to be finicky. These stakeholders are the folks who tend to sit back and wait to see how the project's going before they decide if they're going to support you or not. The animal avatar for these folks is the *flamingo*. Flamingos are fabulously finicky creatures, particularly when it comes to their diet, and they often flock together. You'll need to figure out how to transform them into cheerleaders as soon as possible and keep them away from the saboteurs. A coaching client of mine remembered the F as "on the fence," which is fair too!

MEET STAKEHOLDER GABBY

To understand more about how stakeholders can impact your project, imagine a stakeholder named Gabby. She is very excited about the software project you're leading, because she's been advocating for it to be approved for three years. She thinks she's helping to get other people excited about the project too, by telling everyone who will listen about some of the helpful features that will be included to make their jobs easier.

Unfortunately, since Gabby is not on the team, she is unaware that the project has evolved, and those features were deprioritized in the spirit of getting the core software released on time. Rather than being excited, the people who were all fired up for easier lives are now disappointed, asking a lot of questions and putting pressure on the team to get these features done—without the benefit of the sound reasoning behind the team's prioritization. While Gabby had good intentions, now the project manager has to engage in unexpected damage control activities. Harnessing Gabby's energy and engaging her appropriately, would have helped to avoid this situation. Gabby feels terrible, because instead of being a cheerleader, she accidentally became a saboteur. And some of those finicky fans that were on the fence, turned into saboteurs, too.

Next, let's explore some common stakeholder groups that often pop up in the corporate jungle to help you think through who your stakeholders could be.

FIVE TYPICAL STAKEHOLDER GROUPS

Shareholders – Some people get confused when I talk about stakeholders, and think I'm saying shareholders. Yes, these are totally different words that sound a lot alike. And yes, if you work for a company that has shareholders, then they are ultimately also stakeholders at everything your company does, including your project. By being fiscally responsible and protecting the company reputation, these special stakeholders should be satisfied. Unless your project is directly visible to them, there usually are not too many instances when your project would need to take special action to respond to the concerns of shareholders. If you'd like to be thorough and add this group to your list of stakeholders, it surely won't hurt anything. You can then be sure they don't require any extra attention. And if they do, you'll be ready.

Little "c" customers – I've spent over 20 years working with internal Information Technology (IT) shops. Some IT shops, as well as other shared services inside organizations, talk about serving their customers. This can be confusing. So now I ask, "Is that a small c customer or a BIG C Customer?" Meaning, the little c customer is internal. They get paid by the same company as IT does. My advice is to admit your colleagues aren't really customers at all, even if there is money moving between departments. We should all be on the same team, making sound decisions with the best interests of the total enterprise in mind. I've seen actions tend toward silliness when internal groups think other internal groups are their customers. For instance, too much time spent on making presentations pretty rather than delivering results, and spending the equivalent of $1,000 on a $100 problem, because "the customer is always right" and "I am here to serve." I'd rather use the term "internal partners" (we're all on the same team, remember?) or "end users" in the case of IT.

Big "C" Customers – These are real, paying people or organizations. These are definitely "Customers" with a capital C. Unfortunately, in Projectland, we don't always have access to work with them directly. It is unfortunate, because of a phenomenon that you probably learned in elementary school. Did you ever play the "the whisper down the lane" game? I believe I was in the second grade (the same year I became best friends with the corner for talking too much), when Mr. Schwartz had us stand in a circle. He whispered a sentence to the kiddo on his left, and each person after that had to whisper what they thought they heard to their neighbor. By the time the sentence got back to Mr. Schwartz, it was shorter, completely ridiculous, and not at all what he had said. Thus, I ended up learning another animal-based expression, "Always get the intel from the horse's mouth." If you can, involve actual customers and let everyone hear what they have to say directly. If that is impossible or reputationally dangerous, appoint someone who is customer-savvy to be the customer representative. It's a risk to appoint a representative because no one can really know what someone else is thinking. To reduce this risk, ensure that the representative is really, really good at interpreting the needs, desires, and opinions of the customers, and has a process to get their feedback on a regular basis.

Resource Managers – Many organizations work in a matrix environment where people are pulled together from different departments for a particular project, but still have a manager who is responsible for their human resource needs and their non-project work assignments. We call them "resource managers" (sometimes called department or functional managers) and since they are NOT part of the project, they are stakeholders who often have a very important role in helping the right people be assigned to the right projects at the right time. In fact, in many cases, the resource managers are the ones with the clearest vision of what will be on their people's plate for the foreseeable future. This is particularly true in environments where the same resources are responsible for both operations and project tasks. When I teach this concept to college students, I equate the "resource manager" to the "home room teacher" in high school. The home room teacher takes attendance and can handle general needs, but you'd go to the science teacher for specific guidance on how to win the blue ribbon for your science fair project.

Operations – These are the people responsible for the ongoing maintenance or operation of the product, service, or result your project will deliver. For instance, if the project is to build a bridge, the project team goes upriver when construction is over to build the next bridge. It's up to the painters, light-bulb changers and pylon inspectors, to make sure the bridge stays in good repair for years to come. Identify the operations team as early as possible and figure out how to integrate them into the project at key stages, so that by the end, they can't say they aren't ready to take on the ongoing operations required to maintain your project's product, service, or result. There may even be opportunities to involve them in project tasks, so that they can help you get project work done while also learning. This is a win-win! For instance, you might involve some of the operations team members to be part of testing the new software they will later need to support. Even if the team that's building the thing and then maintaining it is the same, it's good practice to confirm this as early as possible and make sure they'll have enough bandwidth to do a good job supporting its ongoing use. Plus, it's always a good idea to build ways into the project to make maintenance easier. The point is to ensure the stakeholders relying on your product, service, or result will get all the expected benefits and your organization will achieve the highest ROI possible.

CONCLUSION

Now you know more about who stakeholders are, the three surprising kinds, and their corresponding animal avatars: the happy dog, the flamingo, and the snake. You also learned about five typical stakeholder groups. In an upcoming chapter called, "What to Do About

Stakeholders, Especially the Difficult Ones," I'll introduce a thinking tool to help you identify, organize, and figure out what to do about all of your project's stakeholders, so that you can deliver with a high degree of stakeholder satisfaction and achieve that coveted five-star review from at least the important creatures in your version of Projectland.

WHAT'S NEXT?

WOOHOO! You've now met all of the players in Projectland and completed Section II of the book! Roll up your sleeves and check your gear, because this next phase of the journey is where we get 'em on board and ready to rumble.

PRACTICAL PROJECTLAND CHALLENGE

Take Action!

1. Consider your project. Who are the people who might love your project, hate your project, or be somewhere in between?

2. Do any of the typical project stakeholder groups apply to your project?

- Shareholders
- Little "c" customers
- Big "C" Customers
- Resource managers
- Operations

3. Consider stakeholders from past projects.

- Who were cheerleaders? Finicky fans who you turned into cheerleaders? Finicky fans who went the other way? Were

there any saboteurs–whether overt or covert?
- What can you learn from these experiences and apply to current or future projects?

GET 'EM ON BOARD

& READY TO RUMBLE

SECTION THREE
GET 'EM ON BOARD &
READY TO RUMBLE

Now that you have a foundational understanding of Projectland and the creatures you may encounter during your journey, it's time to figure out who you need, how to get them on board, and ultimately get them rowing in the right direction. We'll also cover a few common pitfalls, so that you know what to do if they happen to you. Let's do this!

CHAPTER 10
LOVE THE CREATURES YOU'RE WITH

"If you have a problem, if no one else can help,
and if you can find them, maybe you can hire... the A-Team."
- The A-Team TV Series Opening Monologue (1983-87)

A sking for a friend. I know a woman who is single, owns a home, and wants a backyard oasis. She has two hands and isn't afraid to use a wheelbarrow. Her key stakeholder is a happy dog who is the Chief Officer of Cuteness, but who has yet to grow thumbs. Otherwise, the pup would be recruited to be part of the team.

What would you recommend our friend do? She's probably going to need some help, right? It seems to me that she has two choices: hiring a local contractor or recruiting a crew of very good friends with tools, a pickup truck, and an account at Home Depot.

If you agree with the advice, "you get what you pay for," you would caution our friend to choose her helpers wisely. Do they have the right skills and experience? Do we need to buy or rent equipment, so that it's available when they show up to help? Does she have a budget in mind for this project?

In this chapter, we'll discuss how to identify who you need for your project team, how to evaluate whether you have the right team members, and how to start socializing the project to shore up support.

Advice from musician Stephen Stills is to "love the one you're with," which can also come in handy when you have limited or no options as to who is part of your project. However, you may have more influence than you think regarding choosing your team members! We'll discuss how our animal avatars can help us create a winning team, and how to create your step-by-step plan to recruit your A-team and get them committed to win. Plus, we'll check in with our backyard oasis dreamer to see what happened.

WHEN DO YOU START RECRUITING FOR YOUR TEAM?

Once our lady friend knows WHAT she wants (what is a backyard oasis, anyway?), then the skills she needs to create the key deliverables are usually pretty obvious. For instance, if she wants a butterfly garden, she'll need to do a lot of research herself or consult with a butterfly garden expert or both. This is why defining the scope is helpful to do first. Identify what *it* is that you're creating, and then you'll know *who* you need to create *it*. The scope is the *it*.

Start to recruit and assemble the team as early as possible, because this process generally takes more time than you'd think. If someone is actually sitting around waiting for your call with nothing to do, be shocked! Most folks are in the middle of something else and need to find time in their schedules before they can help you. And that is if they even want to help.

BUT FIRST, CLEARLY DEFINE THE PROJECT

Before you can recruit people, you have work to do to define your project in a way that is compelling enough to convince people to *want* to get involved. In many work cultures, telling people they are on a team can backfire. Even in military and paramilitary organizations, you'd rather have people feeling committed to the cause than muttering under their breath that they don't understand the point.

Remember, a project is a temporary endeavor undertaken to create a unique product, service or result. It's much easier to start recruiting the team once you can explain:

1. Why this project is important (e.g., the problem it needs to solve or the opportunity to seize)
2. Why now (e.g., not next year), and
3. Why it's worth it (i.e., benefits outweigh the cost/effort)

Convince yourself first. Write it down on one page. If it still makes sense, then you may find it useful to identify a friendly feedback-giver or two and ask them to help you make sure your idea is clear and compelling before going to your boss or the requester with the idea.

Note that in many organizations, formal steps are defined to help make sure this happens thoughtfully, because resources are scarce and need to be allocated to the most important work. For example, there could be a process to submit project ideas for consideration, and then the ones that sound promising are required to go through an approval process to be weighed against other exciting project ideas. At a minimum, this process usually includes creating a brief document (e.g., project charter, business case or cost justification) that answers the three questions above. If you're not sure what is required in your organization, ask!

PLAN YOUR A-TEAM WITH HELP FROM THE PROJECTLAND ANIMAL AVATARS

First, you need to figure out the project leadership team. Identify your *one* Project Sponsor, which is represented by the lion, because there can be only one king (or queen!) of the jungle. You also need *one* Project Manager, which is the tiger – not quite the lion, but awfully close. If the project is large or complex, you may also need to recruit Steering Team member(s), to help the big cats be successful. These are represented by broad-vision eagles, wise owls, and giant whales.

Next, you need people to actually do the work. This is your team. Our team member animal avatars (the gazelle, bison, and dolphin) are naturally good team players.

If you haven't read Section II, check it out for inspiration about key characteristics that will help you identify the humans you need to recruit, because of their responsibilities in the organization, their work styles, as well as their specific expertise.

SOCIALIZE YOUR PROJECT TO RALLY LEADERSHIP SUPPORT FIRST

A few years ago, my brother and his buddy were sitting around the big screen TV watching sports and saw a sizzling Outback Steakhouse commercial. They looked at each other, nodded, grabbed car keys and wallets, and started the 45-minute trek to the restaurant. Unfortunately, it usually isn't that easy to convince anyone at work to get moving on a project idea.

In the beginning, there is just an idea. Naturally, whoever had the idea is the most excited about it at first. To transform this idea into something tangible, the person who had the idea often needs to convince others that it is indeed a good idea.

After you've thought through who your ideal project leadership team is, you need to get them on board. Perhaps this is already done, because the sponsor and project manager are obvious. If not, you should take your brief write-up that makes your case about why this project is important, why now is the right time to do it, and why it's worth doing, to your ideal sponsor first. If you're going to be the sponsor, take it to your boss and propose that you be the sponsor. Once you have the sponsor identified and on board, you'll need a project manager.

Please, please, please do not say that you are the sponsor, the project manager, and the SME, unless the project is cleaning your own desk by yourself with your own supplies on your own time.

Consider who the ideal project manager is with the help of our tiger animal avatar. If you have professional project managers in your organization, meaning their title and job responsibilities are all about managing projects, they often do not need any expertise in the subject matter to do a good job, as long as you can get the right team leads and/or SMEs on board. While it never hurts if you have a great pro project manager with the subject matter expertise too, this is less important than most people think. If you don't have professional project managers, or if your project is too small to warrant assigning one, then choose someone who has expertise in the subject matter with good leadership, communication, and problems-solving skills. Review the Top 10 Typical Responsibilities for each role explained in Section II to be sure they are up to the task.

Once the sponsor and project manager are assigned, they can determine whether or not steering team member(s) are needed with the help of "Chapter 6: The Steering Team is Not a Committee: Eagles, Whales, & Owls, Oh My!" If your sponsor knows they need a steering team, even if it is a steering team of one, get these leaders on board next. It is worth taking the time to speak with them, get their feedback, answer their questions, and gain their support, before moving forward with any of the heavy lifting of the project. This is because if you cannot get their support, you're essentially heading toward a Projectland cliff.

Later in this chapter, I'll give you some ideas for how to have recruiting conversations with leaders, as well as what to do if you don't feel you have the support you need to succeed.

Once you have the full leadership team on board, the work of recruiting team members is much easier. Later in the chapter, I'll share more about how to have conversations with resources or resource managers to recruit the team members who will do the work of the project.

WHAT IF THERE ARE CRICKETS?

When you do the important work to think through who you need on your team, and ask, "Who in our organization has these skills? What about key competencies or characteristics that will help us succeed," and all you hear is silence and maybe some crickets chirping in the background, it may be time to ask if there is budget to hire someone on a contract basis to help.

Indeed, going outside your organization and hiring a contractor can be helpful. For instance, if you decide you want a swimming pool at your house, you could choose to do the work yourself on the weekends and recruit some friends to help. (It's a BYOS party! Bring Your Own Shovel, and if you don't have shovels, bring Spoons!) But, if you and your friends aren't pool project pros and you want a quality pool that doesn't leak, you'll probably call a local company with a good reputation for installing pools.

Think about what kind of person you need to help your project go faster (i.e., your gazelle) and if that person exists inside your organization. If the person does not exist, you will want to quickly gain support to acquire the skill from outside the organization, because the procurement process always seems to take more time than anyone could ever predict.

Situations where it makes sense to bring in temporary help typically include:

- If your project is billable to the customer, the extra cost can be offset by the revenue or built into the fee.
- When you have the skills in-house, but the people aren't available.
- The work you need is seasonal.
- The project includes a special flurry of work that the organization simply isn't staffed for.

SHOW ME THE MONEY

In the 1996 romantic comedy, *Jerry Maguire*, the once-cocky sports agent played by Tom Cruise is out of a job, desperate, and calls professional football player, Rod Tidwell, played by Cuba Gooding, Jr. Because he is unhappy with his existing contract, Gooding gyrates and repeats, "Show me the money!", and insists that Maguire scream it back at him.[1] By the way, I love this scene!

To get someone to come play for your team from outside your organization, you too will need someone to show you the money. Be prepared to answer this important question, "Who is going to pay for this?" or "Who's budget is this coming out of?" If you do not have spending authority and/or the funds you need were not pre-approved and sitting in the budget ready for you to spend, you will need to gain the support of either your boss, who may be serving as the project sponsor in the interim, or whomever else has been named as the project sponsor.

If a project sponsor has not been named, you will need to identify who has spending authority for the project, whether that means budget to be spent on external resources or equipment, or on internal labor costs (i.e., allocating people to the project, because, after all, time is money). The person with this spending authority becomes the project sponsor by default if nobody else has been named. Note that the project sponsor may not control all the funding, but they generally are responsible for coordinating and influencing budget owners from other departments. Often, the collective budget owners make up the steering team, and the project sponsor is the accountable leader spearheading the project.

If you do not get support for the outside resource, then is the project really that important to the powers that be? Probably not. This is when you'll benefit from having an important tradeoff discussion. It could go something like this...

"Your request for a contractor was denied. I'm sorry, Sally," says Sponsor Damien[2], not looking sorry at all.

Savvy Sally replies, "Hmmm. That's a shame. My understanding was that the project was a priority."

Damien starts acting like shuffling papers is important work and says, "Well, it is a priority. You're just going to have to figure it out."

Harnessing some big cat courage and determination, Sally smiles. "You know I love a challenge." She pauses to let that sink in. Then she frames the issue.

"It seems to me," she adds, "we need to accept the fact that without the benefit of anyone who has ever done this before on the team, the project will likely take longer and the quality will suffer. What I'm hearing is that if our project were to build an in-ground swimming pool in the backyard, instead of hiring a pool contractor, we're supposed to call in all the neighbors and dig it with spoons? Or, perhaps we need to adjust our vision of swimming laps in luxury, and buy an inflatable kiddie pool instead. My point is that we might need to go back to the drawing board a bit before we move forward, since our plan was predicated upon procuring an expert. Now I'm feeling like we'll need an A-team with some resourceful, savvy, creative, determined creatures, and many of them are tied up on other work. There are tradeoffs that may be needed. Let me go think about our options. Could I come back to you tomorrow with some ideas and ask for your advice?"

"Uh. Sure," responds Sponsor Damien, wondering what just happened, while Savvy Sally walks away with her chin up, already thinking about a few options, such as:

- Delaying the start of the project until internal resources are available
- Pausing other lower-priority work to free-up resources for this higher priority project
- Allowing the schedule to extend to accommodate using small percentages of people's time
- Accepting the risk of lower quality
- Taking a phased approach by starting small with what you CAN do now
- Changing the solution (e.g., volunteering at the local swimming pool in exchange for swim time rather than the inground Instagram-worthy backyard pool of your dreams)

Go back to your sponsor in the timeframe you said you would with clear options to discuss. Ask for advice on which options might be worth exploring further. If one or more get a positive nod, great! If not, don't fret and keep reading.

WHO DO YOU RECRUIT?

Once you've, at a minimum, convinced *yourself* that the project is worth doing now, and you think you could convince others to join you on your quest, I suspect that you will want the best team members you can get.

At work, don't be surprised if everyone wants the same top people and if those people aren't always available when you need them. You'll need to do what you can to maneuver the work around their schedules or find other people who have the bandwidth to help.

In addition to the skills you need, you also want people who will be good team players. If you follow sports or Hollywood, you probably have heard about superstar athletes or actors who are difficult to deal with. When I have a choice, I'll take someone with a solid set of skills who enjoys being part of a team over a superstar prima donna with an attitude problem. I don't want to sign up for the tedious job of removing all of the red M&Ms from the bag. Projectland is hard enough already.

HOW DO YOU RECRUIT THE A-TEAM?

If you have a process in your organization that needs to be followed to get the right resources assigned to your project, please do follow it. Whether or not there is a clear process, it often includes the 3 'C's of Projectland: Communicate, Communicate, Communicate.

Earlier, in "Chapter 9: Three Surprising Kinds of Stakeholders," I introduced the concept that in a matrix environment, there is often an important stakeholder group that we call Resource Managers. Often in recruiting the team, these folks help make sure that the right people get assigned to the right projects at the right time. You or your project sponsor may need to speak with one or more Resource Managers who have the people with the skills you need for your project. Rather than saying, "I need Bob." You may say, "I need an expert Bobcat operator in the Spring. I've worked with Bob before, and I thought he was great! I'd love to get to work with him again if you could make him available. This project is for the Smiths, who are very particular, and they have a tricky property. If Bob isn't available, we'll need someone else who can handle those conditions." Being open and clear with project information will help you get the right person.

BUT, WHAT IF YOU GET THE B-, C- OR Z-TEAM (AKA HOW TO LOVE THE CREATURES YOU'RE WITH)?

Whether you have the A-team or the Z-team, let's face facts. You're at work. You probably don't love everyone equally, or maybe not at all. Certain creatures, like rowdy roosters right outside your window when you're trying to sleep, have irritating quirks. Perhaps the woman down the hall makes you jump every time she sneezes. Or, one of your colleagues gets a little too close for comfort for every conversation. There's not much of a point in getting angry with and having a conversation with the rooster about its behavior. Roosters are loud and obnoxious. It's just how they are. You'll have to decide if addressing the humans about their quirks is worth your breath or not. Or perhaps you're just having "one of those days." Either way, remember, this is why they pay you to show up. Take a deep breath, perhaps chuckle to yourself at the absurdity, and resolve to do your best all day anyway. Chin up, buttercup. You will get through this.

We discussed how every project is unique. So, is every human. And while you wish Sneezy would lower the decibel-level a notch or ten, maybe she loves that coffee shop around the corner, and fuzzy bunny slippers too. Try to have a friendly conversation and find some common ground. If Grumpy was assigned to your team, make it your secret mission to elicit even a hint of a smirk. Not everyone is as ambitious as you are. Not everyone learns the same way you do. Not everyone cares about spelling and grammar in text messages, either. The first step is to figure out and accept who you have. What are their supposed strengths that will be helpful? What are characteristics (real or perceived) that could be harmful to your project? Play to their strengths and work around their individual weaknesses and look across the team to make sure that, collectively, you have the skills and talent that you need to succeed. Figure out how to work with the people you have available to you. It's like when I come home late from traveling and I have to figure out how to make a meal out of the three remaining edible things I happen to have handy. Sometimes you have to make do.

EVALUATE WHETHER YOU HAVE THE RIGHT TEAM MEMBERS

After you've figured out who you have to work with you, double check your scope and make sure you have a commitment to get all of the resources (e.g., humans, equipment, supplies, budget, etc.) you need.

BE A LEADER. BE RESOURCEFUL.

Let's get back to our project with Sponsor Damien. Can you get the resources you need (A-team or otherwise) or is it a lost cause? Particularly in larger organizations, you probably have more influence and resources available than you think. Even in start-ups, you might find the perfect person on Fiverr to help for a reasonable cost.

If you go back to Damien, you might say, "Okay, I figured out that Grumpy is great at risk management and Sneezy is super at documentation. It would be helpful if we had someone who was an expert Bobcat operator, so we don't have to dig with spoons. Can we ask around the office to see if anyone is a machine head who could spare some time for us?" If Damien really does want this project (and you!) to succeed, the answer will be, "Sounds good." And perhaps he'll even add, "Let me know if you need any support."

PREPARE FOR BRIEF RECRUITING CONVERSATIONS

At this point, you should know who you need to speak with to recruit your team. Remember, your team must include one sponsor and could include steering team members too. Give yourself the best chance at getting a "yes" to your request for the very best resources that can be made available to you.

Here are some pro tips to having positive recruiting conversations:

1. Plan. Do not make a surprise request.
2. If you're recruiting someone above your level, invite their peer in your part of the organization to join you. For

instance, if you're a project sponsor and you need to recruit steering team members who are at your boss's level in the organization, ask your boss to join you.

3. Request 30 minutes or less with the appropriate people (e.g., resource managers, potential steering team members, external recruiters) by finding time on their calendars. Do not make this a giant meeting. Individual conversations are usually best and are also easier to schedule.

4. In the meeting notice, include brief project information, so that they can read it ahead of time, and so that you can easily find it when it's time for the meeting. Also include your specific request for their help in the meeting notice, so that they aren't wondering what you need from them. For instance, "I'd like to discuss the possibility of you engaging as a Steering Team member, given your leadership role in Finance in South America." Or if the discussion is with a resource manager, "I'd like to discuss engaging a SME from your team to help us build the next generation of popular product X. I worked with Emilie on a previous project, and I'd love to work with her again, or someone with similar skills who shares her terrific 'everything is figure-outable' attitude." This will allow them to consider the request along with their people's bandwidth and prepare questions before your meeting.

5. Be friendly. Ask and answer questions respectfully. Ask for their advice to help you recruit the right people. Do not be pushy. This can backfire. You don't want to get your project stalled or canceled before it has even begun. Nor do you want to spawn new saboteurs who might otherwise become cheerleaders.

6. Follow up within 24 hours of the meeting with a sincere thank you and a recap of your understanding of the decisions, next steps, and other helpful elements of the conversation.

If you haven't already guessed it, the homeowner lady with the dog is me. I'd been dreaming about a butterfly garden for a long time, as well as researching butterflies and their corresponding favorite plants in my area. Fortunately, a dear friend of mine has a pickup truck and an account at Home Depot and introduced me to his new boyfriend whom we dubbed "My Butterfly Guy" during a late-night business incubator idea-fest. What good fortune that they were happy to help my butterfly garden dreams come true, and even had some extra time on their hands! Perhaps you've heard the advice to "strike while the iron is hot." I decided that while I had the interest of the perfect people to help me, it was a sign to prioritize getting this dream project done, even though it was July in Florida. (Holy hotness!)

WHEN THE CRICKETS STRIKE AGAIN

In Ed Yourdon's book, *Death March*, he made the case that if a project has less than a 50% chance of succeeding in any key area, it's up to project leadership to recommend NOT leading the team into a situation where they are likely marching toward failure. Do not set your team up to fail from the start.

If at any point, you don't feel you have support, it's best to openly discuss not moving forward rather than trying to push a boulder uphill in the mud. Perhaps now isn't the best time due to other competing priorities, and your energy would be better spent on something that does have support.

Reasonable professionals make decisions for the greater good of the organization. Unreasonable professionals throw tantrums like two-year-olds or are overly relentless. Determine if this is the hill you will stake your job on or not. If it is, realize that irritating your version of Sponsor Damien, could be a career-limiting move. If not, back down graciously, and respectfully ask when might be a good time to revisit prioritizing your project (e.g., next fiscal year, after large project X is stable, after the holidays, etc.).

Then, package all of the work you've done so far on the project and put it in a handy place to dust it off again later, along with a reminder on your calendar for the agreed-upon time.

If the powers that be indicate that this project will never be supported, be gracious and grateful that you didn't waste any additional energy on it. Note your lessons learned and thank them for their time.

DO *NOT* ASSUME THIS ONE THING

When I train people to write solid project charters, business cases, cost justifications, or whatever their organization calls the write-up required to get a project approved, I always ask them to include at least this one assumption: "Resources will be available per the schedule."

An assumption is something we think is true, but there is no proof[3]. At the start of the project, when it's just an idea, you have to make this assumption, or you can't move forward. As you start to learn exactly who is assigned to your project, you need to also find out their actual availability to work on your project. Often, people are not 100% dedicated to your project, so this becomes a real factor in creating a realistic project schedule. You either get them when you need them, or you need to make sure there is agreement to work the project schedule around when they are available.

For instance, our butterfly garden project couldn't start until we acquired the special plants we needed and all of us had the same weekend off work so we could go together to get the truckload of dirt. Supply chain issues for special equipment may cause your project to be delayed months. The team members you need may be out of the office enjoying Chinese New Year, relaxing on the French Riviera in August, taking a month to get married in India, or 50% dedicated to another project.

Be sure to consider availability, set expectations with resources and their managers, and plan accordingly. When you consider actual availability, the project could take weeks or months longer than if everything was lined up and ready to go at the start. The question will be, do you get everything lined up, or do you get started with what you can do now? Consider what is right for your project and its goals.

CONCLUSION

In case you're wondering, my friends and I had fun creating the first phase of my backyard butterfly garden, making memories and providing an ongoing source of smiles. Luckily for me, they are great team players who aren't allergic to sweating up a storm.

That's what I hope for you too. When you recruit team members who are good, hard-working team players, and let them know how happy you are that they're joining you on your trek through Projectland, you can set yourselves up for a great experience.

WHAT'S NEXT?

In the next chapter, we'll dive into what to do about stakeholders, especially the difficult ones.

PRACTICAL PROJECTLAND CHALLENGE

Take Action!

1. Are you ready to recruit your team?

- Do you have a clear enough idea about the project to brief someone and get them excited? Can you explain: Why is this project important, why now, and why is it worth it?
- Do you know what *it* (also known as the scope) is that you're creating, building or delivering, so that you can identify the key skills and experience, equipment, etc., that you need to create/build/deliver *it*?
- Do you know the appropriate process to follow in your organization to recruit people for your project? For example,

do you need to have the project officially approved first, before you go speak with resource managers?

2. When you look around the organization for the skills, equipment, and chutzpah that you need to get the job done, does your quest for A-team level players come up short?

- Do you need to go outside the organization to procure who and what you need to succeed?
- If yes, do you know the answer to the inevitable question, "Who's paying for this?"
- Do you know what the procurement process is?
- Do you have approval to move forward and spend money or allocate people's time?
- Do you need to go back to the drawing board and redefine what you can do with the internal players available to you?
- Are there hidden people in your organization with the skills you need to succeed?

3. Do you feel you have the support and resources needed to succeed? If not, review the section called, "When the Crickets Strike Again," and determine your path forward to gracefully close this project before you waste more time and energy than it's worth.

4. Are you ready to set up some brief meetings to start discussing your project and asking for the resources you need? If so, check out the six pro tips mentioned in the "Prepare for Brief Recruiting Conversations" section above!

CHAPTER 11
WHAT TO DO ABOUT STAKEHOLDERS, ESPECIALLY THE DIFFICULT ONES

"I love me some me."
- Terrell Owens, American Football Hall of Famer

Much like this chapter's opening quote by the American football star, "T.O.," who was notorious for being an over-the-top egomaniac, some stakeholders have a serious case of "What's In It For Me" (WIIFM) syndrome.

Remember, stakeholders are the people who may love your project, hate your project, or be somewhere in between. While the team has a definite stake in the project too, we refer to the people OUTSIDE of your core project team when we use the term *stakeholders*.

Since our goal is to deliver projects with a high degree of stakeholder satisfaction, we need to create a plan and take action to address their varying needs and expectations throughout the project. If you are new to Projectland, you likely need to care about this more than you suspect. Most newbies skip this step altogether and find later how detrimental that miss can be.

As the saying, "the court of public opinion," goes, how key people experience and will remember your project matters. Your project can deliver the perfect product, service, or result, and your team can even deliver it on time, on budget, on scope, and on quality, but if you've upset a lot of important stakeholders along the way, the project could still be deemed a failure. Don't let this common Projectland trap happen to you!

Let's dive into the thinking tool that our project gurus use, as well as five practical steps to help you deliver with a high degree of stakeholder satisfaction. For small projects, getting through all these steps may take you only fifteen minutes and avoid ages of agony. For larger projects, it will take a little longer, and I trust you will find it to be time well spent.

MEET YOUR NEW FRIEND SAMM: THE THINKING TOOL

Now I'd like you to meet SAMM, our *Stakeholder Analysis and Management Matrix*, because SAMM is here to help you think through who your stakeholders are, what they care about, and what to do about it. SAMM is a tool for private use by the project leadership team (you'll see why later). You can download your own copy for free from the Project Guru Press website (projectgurupress.com/meettheplayers/tools).

Stakeholders, like I mentioned, are the people outside of your project who might love your project, hate your project, or be somewhere in between. And here is where we privately list all of those people, think about their top concerns, and create a plan to manage them. Usually managing stakeholder expectations is done through a whole lot of communicating. This is why the Communications Plan is located on the same page as the SAMM. Be sure to add to your work plans (e.g., scope, schedule, etc.) any communication or other deliverables that you need to create to help you manage the stakeholders. Meanwhile, here are the five steps you can take to help foster stakeholder satisfaction:

STEP 1: IDENTIFY ALL STAKEHOLDERS

Your first step is to identify all the people and organizations with an interest in your project. That's right. It's time to name names. If you're using SAMM, you'll be listing stakeholders in the first few columns: Stakeholder Group, Subgroup, and Contact Point/Stakeholder Name.

Don't worry about filling out every cell. Do worry about identifying as many stakeholders as you can. The thing to remember at this point is to cast a wide net. In fact, the wider the better. Name all the groups and individual people you expect may be impacted or could perceive themselves to be impacted by your project. Don't concern yourself with evaluating them yet, because in the next steps you will analyze and decide what to do about them. Instead, rattle them all off quickly and include everyone you can think of at this point. You can also reference "Chapter 9: Three Surprising Kinds of Stakeholders" for a reminder of some typical stakeholders, so that you can determine if they apply to your project.

Let's explore an example. We've mentioned the case of building a backyard swimming pool a few times now. So let's dive deeper into this situation (see what I did there?). Let's say the Smith family wants a pool in their backyard. In this case, Grandma Smith might be an individual stakeholder or a member of the "family members" group if she has a keen interest in the pool and/or any concerns. The neighbors are likely a stakeholder group as well, since the pool and its construction may impact them.

But wait! Since not all neighbors are created equal, it can be helpful to break them into "subgroups," such as "reasonable neighbors" and "negative neighbors." You should specifically note the nosy, bon-bon-eating-daytime-soap-opera-watching Mrs. Jones next door in the negative neighbor subgroup, because you anticipate that she could become a real problem.

In this pool example, "the government" is another good stakeholder group to consider, since you'll likely need a permit. You might not know exactly who you'll be dealing with yet, so you can list the subgroup as "permit office" and name names later.

As you work to identify stakeholder groups, subgroups, and known named stakeholders and capture them in the first few columns of the SAMM, simply do your best and cast a wide net. You can always add to this list later as you think of or discover more stakeholders.

Here's what our SAMM starts to looks like during Step 1:

	Stakeholder Identification		
ID #	**Stakeholder Group**	**SubGroup**	**Contact Point / Stakeholder name**
1	Family		Grandma Smith
2	Neighbors	Negative Nextdoor	Mrs. Jones
3	Neighbors	Reasonable	Bill & Ted LaVerne & Shirley
4	Government	Permit Office	TBD

Figure 11.1 - SAMM Step 1

STEP 2: ORGANIZE AND ANALYZE STAKEHOLDERS

This next part of the exercise often feels uncomfortable to everyone who wishes to believe the best in people (which is such a beautiful attitude!). However, in Projectland it can be detrimental to ignore the real possibility that some people only have their best interests in mind (i.e., WIIFM syndrome strikes again), which may be counter to your project goals.

As we discussed in "Chapter 9: Three Surprising Kinds of Stakeholders," it can be helpful to organize Stakeholders into three categories:

- *Cheerleaders* love your project and will do everything to help. Sometimes, they may think they're being helpful but end up meddling. **Think: the happy dog who gets underfoot when you're cooking, and a yummy morsel drops on the floor.**
- *Finicky fans* are the ones who may wait to decide if they're going to be supportive *or not* until they see how well your project's going. We want to move them off the fence and into cheerleader mode and keep them away from the saboteurs. **Think: flamingos, which often flock together.**
- *Saboteurs* are folks who hate your project and may attempt to derail it. (My young professional learners call them haters.) **Think: the snake in the grass that can jump up and bite you when you're trampling around in its happy meadow.**

**We need to know where they are and create a plan, so they
don't sabotage our project.**

After the Stakeholder Group, Subgroup and Contact Point/Stakeholder Name columns have some content in the SAMM, it's time to leverage the next column, labeled C/F/S. This is the private place to mark each stakeholder in the list as a Cheerleader, Finicky Fan, or Saboteur. I say private, because we don't want anyone besides the project manager, sponsor, and maybe another trusted leader or two seeing this categorization. I highly recommend NOT defining these letters in this tool. We don't want to find out what would happen if someone sees their name and realizes they were labeled as a saboteur. Keeping the spreadsheet secure and confidential is critical here, so that you don't suffer any more wrath from the S's than necessary. Villains are the heroes of their own story, after all.

At the same time that you're thinking about who might be a cheerleader, finicky fan, or saboteur, you should be thinking about WHY that is. This is a great time to note in the next column of your SAMM what you expect their top concerns for the project could be. For instance, what might be the top concern for Mrs. Jones? It could be that she doesn't want to be inconvenienced at all, including noise. Write that down. What might the top concern be for Grandma? Perhaps it is that you finally get the backyard oasis of your dreams, and that it's safe for both her grandkids and her Pinochle-playing friends alike.

If you're working on a critical project, you may even want to task a team member with interviewing stakeholders to directly get the scoop on their concerns. Though this is the best and most accurate way to do it, it may feel like a luxury that your project can't afford. If that's the case, just do your best! Your best effort is most certainly better than nothing, which is unfortunately what many projects get in this area.

Here's what our SAMM starts to look like after Step 2:

	Stakeholder Identification				Analysis
ID #	Stakeholder Group	SubGroup	Contact Point / Stakeholder name	C F S	Stakeholder's Top Concerns
1	Family		Grandma Smith	C	Wants to help and is worried about safety for both grandkids and Pinochle-playing friends.
2	Neighbors	Negative Nextdoor	Mrs. Jones	S	Something new to complain about. YAY! Noise from the project might disrupt daytime soap operas.
3	Neighbors	Reasonable	Bill & Ted LaVerne & Shirley	F	Don't want to be inconvenienced.
4	Government	Permit Office	TBD	F	Your project isn't my priority. Don't be mean or you go to the bottom of the pile.

Figure 11.2 - SAMM Step 2

STEP 3: DETERMINE HOW BEST TO MANAGE THEM

So far, we've identified and organized our stakeholders into groups, subgroups, three key categories, and noted their likely concerns. Step three in assuring stakeholder satisfaction is to determine how best to manage the expectations of the identified stakeholders throughout the project, based on their likely perspective (C/F/S) and specific concerns. You'll write down your ideas for action in the next column called "Planned Management Response." Once your sponsor has agreed, these ideas collectively are your initial plan to give your team the best shot at delivering with a high degree of stakeholder satisfaction. You should also continue to update this thinking tool throughout the project.

To illustrate how this works, let's strategize to help the Smith family, who wants a swimming pool.

Grandma Smith is a big fan of the project, eager to help and even has a Pinterest board with all of her ideas. She's a cheerleader. To make sure that Grandma feels loved and doesn't meddle, Mrs. Smith could:

- Spend an evening with her and her Pinterest board.

- Share Grandma's ideas with the contractor and give her credit.
- Make sure the contractor knows direction isn't to come from Grandma, even if she sounds convincing, and to direct any confusion to Mrs. Smith.

Do you see how these are all practical actions that can be taken and will help Grandma continue to be a cheerleader?

As suggested earlier, one stakeholder group represents the Smiths' neighbors. It's good that we already broke that group down further into the negative neighbors and the reasonable ones, because we'll manage each subgroup uniquely. For instance, our potential named saboteur, Mrs. Jones, is home all day eating bonbons and loves to complain to everyone who will listen. Noise from the project might disrupt her daytime soap operas. She may go as far as calling the police with a noise complaint. So, we may recommend that Mrs. Smith visit Mrs. Jones to:

- Explain that the project will start soon and any noise should stop by evening.
- Suggest that Mrs. Jones call her right away if there are any problems and make a point to write down Mrs. Smith's mobile phone number.
- Invite the Jones family to the grand opening party in gratitude for being such good, understanding neighbors.

Plus, she should plan to check in with Mrs. Jones a few times throughout the project. Notice all the extra work we're suggesting here, since Mrs. Jones is a potential saboteur.

Luckily, most of the other neighbors are reasonable, but they could become unreasonable if they are inconvenienced. So, Mrs. Smith could:

- Ask the contractor to be sure to park vehicles on her lot and not in the street.
- Make a point to chat up these neighbors, ask them to call directly with issues, invite them to the party, and, most

of all…

- Keep them away from Mrs. Jones! (I'm kidding, sorta.)

Take great care before you decide to ignore any stakeholders, because good ideas and issues can come from anywhere. Double-check the top concerns and your planned management responses with your sponsor, including the possible response of "doing nothing" (which is a legitimate strategy in some cases). Literally type that the planned management response is to "Do nothing. Wait and see." Otherwise, if issues arise later in the project, your sponsor may wonder why nothing was done to prevent it.

Once you're done with your initial list, you can sort the stakeholders and see all of the C, F, and S stakeholders grouped together. Then, you can examine each category as a group and think about what they have in common and what strategies you can employ to manage them. For example, you could ask your cheerleaders to become super users or change ambassadors. They could help get the word out about your project and work directly with people to prepare for the change that your project will bring. Plan to give them something to do wherever they can be helpful, otherwise they could decide to do something that is detrimental, even if it's unintended. Remember Gabby from Chapter 9?

You could plan to include a mix of cheerleaders and finicky fans in a focus group. You could decide to individually interview potential saboteurs to understand their concerns further. The mob movie adage, "Keep your friends close and your enemies closer," can be very helpful here! In fact, what might feel like critical feedback when first received can challenge the project team to make the project's product, service, or result even better. Without this alternative perspective, you could miss an important opportunity that makes all the difference.

Here are the first few rows of what our SAMM could look like after Step 3:

Stakeholder Identification					Analysis	
ID #	Stakeholder Group	SubGroup	Contact Point / Stakeholder name	C F S	Stakeholder's Top Concerns	Planned Mgmt Respons
1	Family		Grandma Smith	C	Wants to help and is worried about safety for both grandkids and Pinochle-playing friends.	Mrs. Smith will spend an evening with her and her Pinterest board. Listen and share the photos with design elements with the contractor and give her credit. Privately discuss with the contractor that direction isn't to come from Grandma, even if she sounds convincing, and to direct any confusion to Mrs. Smith to provide clarity.
2	Neighbors	Negative Nextdoor	Mrs. Jones	S	Something new to complain about. YAY! Noise from the project might disrupt daytime soap operas.	Bake cookies, make sure she has Mrs. Smith's phone number and invite the Jones Family to the grand opening party.
3	Neighbors	Reasonable	Bill & Ted LaVerne & Shirley	F	Don't want to be inconvenienced.	Ask contractor to park vehicles on the Smith lot. Make sure they have Mrs. Smith's phone number and invite them to the grand opening party.
4	Government	Permit Office	TBD	F	Your project isn't my priority. Don't be mean or you go to the bottom of the pile.	Hire a contractor with a lot of experience and good reputation with the local government.

Figure 11.3 - SAMM Step 3

Finally, when you've completed this exercise, step back and ask, "Are these all of the concerns that people will have? Are these the right ways to address them?" Generally, the answer to that last question is "YES!"—after you complete the next step.

STEP 4: DEVELOP A COMPREHENSIVE COMMUNICATION PLAN

You can best serve stakeholders and your team through great communication. So, ensure all necessary stakeholders are covered in the communication plan. This thinking tool works side-by-side with the SAMM, which is why it is to the right on the same page. Think: "The Communication Plan is SAMM's right-hand."

In the Communication Plan, we include a number of prompts for different types of communication that you may wish to consider and determine if they're applicable to your project and stakeholders. To ensure it's comprehensive, we address communications related to both the project team and the stakeholders. Types of communication deliverables you could include are:

- Internal team meetings, enabled by thinking tools
- Sponsor Status meetings, enabled by a written status report
- Steering Team meetings, enabled by a written status report and chaired by the sponsor
- "Town hall" or "all hands" meetings to present key information and address questions
- Status information from the team to the project manager (e.g., via time reporting, task tracking, and/or verbal updates)
- Status reports from the project manager to the sponsor
- General stakeholder awareness emails at key points in the project
- Senior management awareness updates at key points in the project
- Posters, flyers, or other digital, visible announcements for awareness campaigns
- A project website where stakeholders can go for official updates
- Stakeholder satisfaction surveys
- Focus groups

You can add your organization's typical communication tools to your SAMM to ensure they prompt your thinking for this and future projects. Once you identify the communication deliverables, think through the following, which are represented as columns in the Communication Plan:

- Key messages
- Target audience
- Delivery method (e.g., pre-read email and meeting)
- Delivery frequency (e.g., weekly)
- Owner (e.g., team lead, project manager, sponsor)
- Draft due (i.e., date)
- Done (i.e., date)
- Comments (i.e., anything that might trigger a helpful memory like – "Use format from Project X")

Again, you can download the Communication Plan thinking tool (found next to the SAMM by scrolling to the right in the same sheet) from the Project Guru Press website (projectgurupress.com/meettheplayers/tools).

STEP 5: INCLUDE STAKEHOLDER MANAGEMENT TASKS IN THE SCHEDULE

Add communication deliverables to your Work Breakdown Structure (WBS), which defines your scope clearly, and project schedule, which defines when the deliverables are needed and assigns resources to deliver them. Determine how to ensure the communications are high quality. If you need to add people or things to help, be sure to adjust your resource plan and budget too.

For instance, on very large projects, I've needed an entire team dedicated to preparing people for the change, which I've called the "Change, Communication, & Training (CCT)" Team. Their deliverables and schedule tended to be closely linked to the project's product deliverables, so whenever those product deliverables wiggled, a great deal of communication with the CCT team leader was important to help

CCT project team members adjust their work plans to keep everyone focused and productive.

CONCLUSION

You're now more prepared than most professional project managers to deliver your project with a high degree of stakeholder satisfaction and win in "the court of public opinion." By leveraging the side-by-side pro thinking tools, SAMM and the Communication Plan, you can identify who your stakeholders are, organize them into three fun categories, and create a practical plan for how to manage them.

WHAT'S NEXT?

In our next stop on our journey through Projectland, you will learn one of the most surprising and frequent team traps, and powerful tips for climbing out of it. While this lesson is brief, it is so critical and common that it deserves its own chapter.

PRACTICAL PROJECTLAND CHALLENGE

Put your knowledge to the test! The five steps above may seem like a lot, but so does riding a bike. Just jump on the seat and start peddling! With some practice, you'll get more comfortable communicating with all levels of the organization. Plus, these thinking tools will help you have a great conversation that leads to delivering your project with a high degree of stakeholder satisfaction.

Take Action!

1. If you're the sponsor, you ultimately own the plan. Request a meeting with your project manager and key trusted leaders to go through this exercise. You may request that they draft it before the meeting, so you don't have to be part of the initial sausage-making experience. But be sure to taste-test it

and provide input, because you may have insights the team isn't privy to.

2. Ensure the project leadership team plans to identify project stakeholders, organize them into the three fun categories, write down what their stakeholders' top concerns are, and create a plan to manage those stakeholders' engagement. Remember to keep your SAMM confidential and secure.

3. Introduce yourself to the SAMM and scroll to the right to find the communication plan. Consider what communications will help to deliver the project with a high degree of stakeholder satisfaction. If you're the project manager, determine what adjustments you need to make to the scope, quality, budget, resources, and schedule plans. Review this with your sponsor to be sure you're in alignment, and then make the agreed-upon changes.

4. If you're a team member and not sure if your project leadership team has a plan to deliver with a high degree of stakeholder satisfaction, talk to your project manager and feel free to share the ideas in this book! They should welcome your input.

5. If you are a stakeholder, and you want to help the project succeed or you're concerned about it, see the project manager.

CHAPTER 12
GET READY FOR THE STORM: TEAMING IS A PROCESS, TOO

> "Talent wins games, but teamwork
> and intelligence wins championships."
> - Michael Jordan,[1] Pro Basketball Star, Olympian, & Billionaire

"Dawn, I need to see you in my office now," grumbled my C-suite project sponsor.

I entered and shut the door.

"What is going on with the team?" he said in a tone resembling a low growl. "They don't seem to be getting along well."

I replied calmly, "It feels to me like they're in 'storming' mode now, which is actually a good thing, because it means we can get them up to the performing mode soon."

He looked at me with a semi-confused and still grumbly expression. I tentatively asked, "Have you heard of the teaming process: Forming, Storming, Norming, Performing, and Adjourning?"

He briefly shook his head no.

"Well, it's real and normal. The idea is that in the beginning, when people meet each other, they shake hands, smile, and try to be on their best behavior to make a good first impression. That's 'Forming.' Then, when the team starts to get into the work, they let their guard down a bit because they're more concerned with solving problems and so on.

Reality tends to strike and, of course, the pressure is real on this project. So, they start having conflicts. That's 'Storming.'"

He nodded. He knew. The pressure was real for all of us.

Continuing, I said, "I already asked the team to happy hour on Friday at that little restaurant across the street, so they can start to get to know each other as humans and shake off the storming part that's brewing. Getting everyone out of the office, relaxing together, and having a few laughs usually does the trick to help us get the team into 'norming' and up to 'performing' more quickly. Of course, you're welcome to stop in! I'm sure the team would appreciate it."

He started to relax, and I saw a glimmer of a smile.

"Ok. I'll try," he said. "You promise this is normal, then."

"Yes, absolutely. We'll get through it. We have a good team here."

Good sponsors need to feel confident that the project manager they're relying on to manage the day-to-day has the circus under control. Fortunately, this exchange helped my sponsor feel that I did. Indeed, the team quickly progressed to the Performing stage, and ultimately did great work.

This is just another example of when the human element can be tricky in Projectland. So, let's explore the teaming process phenomenon a bit further so that you are prepared for this uncomfortable, yet entirely normal, situation.

PSYCHOLOGY IN PROJECTLAND

Psychologist Bruce Tuckman came up with the memorable phrase "forming, storming, norming, and performing" in 1965 to describe the path that teams follow on their way to high performance.

In 1977, he and Mary Ann Jensen added a fifth stage to the model, *Adjourning*, sometimes referred to as *Mourning*. In Projectland, we especially need to add Adjourning/Mourning to the end of the process, because projects end.

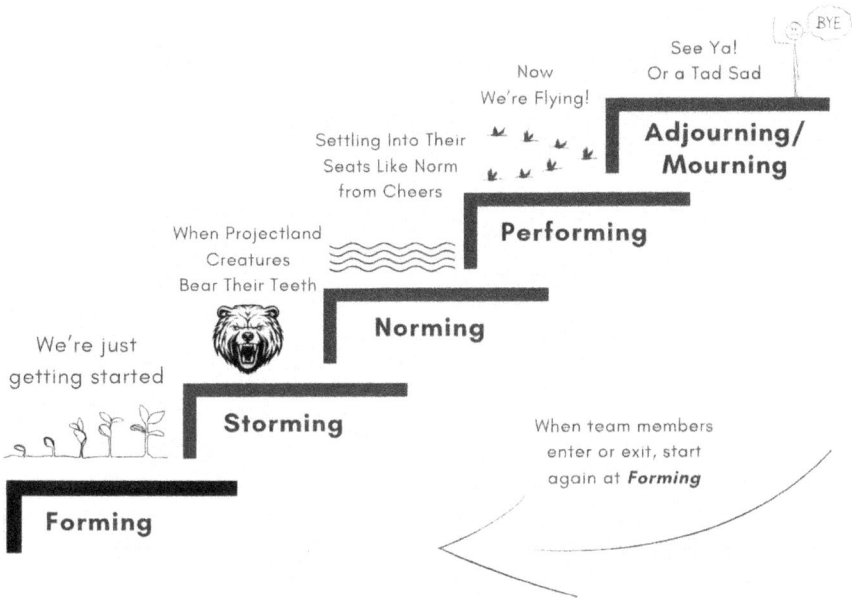

Figure 12.1 – The Projectland Teaming Process

Let's briefly talk about each stage to help you understand how this applies to Projectland.

FORMING – WE'RE JUST GETTING STARTED

At the start of the project, everyone is trying to figure out their role, how they fit, and what to expect from everyone else. Making the roles clear and encouraging friendly interaction among the full team—leadership and team members alike—can help to establish relationships and open communication channels that will be needed later. If you only have budget to get a team together two times during a project, spending budget right at the beginning to get everyone in the right seats and aligned toward the goal is worth it, as it generally saves time and headaches in the long run. This could mean a kickoff meeting with the full team and leadership, more detailed scoping and planning work with the team, a team presentation of that work back to the sponsor and the steering team (if appropriate) for feedback, and some meals together, preferably paid for by the project budget.

As for the second time to spend budget on getting the team together, we'll revisit that later in this chapter when we talk about the Performing stage.

WARNING: Regarding the five stages of team development, every time a new team member is added or one leaves, the team starts back at the beginning, because they have to "re-form" as a team. This is why teams that can keep all of their team members together tend to be more successful over the long-term.

Imagine a rowing team. This is when everyone is figuring out where to sit, which direction their boat is going, and grabbing the oars. And if they accidentally grab the wrong ones, someone will politely point it out.

STORMING – WHEN PROJECTLAND CREATURES BARE THEIR TEETH

Just like it sounds, *Storming* is when tensions rise and, as the saying goes, "the gloves come off." Many project people have not heard of the teaming process, so when the team is in storming mode, they're thinking, "Oh no, what did I sign up for! This project is going to be terrible!" But when they find out about this framework, and that this is normal, they often breathe a sigh of relief. Then, they will make an effort to push through it and move through *Norming* and get up to *Performing*. The framework can give them hope and the motivation to keep going. So, when you sense a storm is brewing, it's okay and sometimes very helpful to observe aloud, "It seems we might be in Storming mode right now. That's good and normal! What can we do to reconnect and realign as humans, so that we can get through the storm and onto the greener pastures of Performing sooner?"

This is exactly what helped the scenario illustrated in the exchange between my project sponsor and me at the beginning of the chapter.

If you are a team member or stakeholder sensing this situation, you can also speak to the project manager, because their role is to help get the team to move through the stages and up to Performing as quickly as possible.

For a rowing team, this is when they're trying to figure out the pace, getting annoyed at the coxswain in the front who is yelling at them, getting occasionally out of sync with the rest of the crew, and starting to feel the burn and wondering what's for lunch.

NORMING – SETTLING INTO THEIR SEATS LIKE NORM FROM CHEERS

After effort is made to get through the Storming stage and realign, the team usually starts to get more comfortable with each other and settle into their roles with more confidence. In the award-winning American sitcom, Cheers, the character called Norm Peterson became famous for making a grand entrance and settling into his seat like he owned the place.[2]

For a rowing team, this is when they're getting into a nice rhythm and starting to feel like maybe, just maybe, they can do this together.

This is a critical point where the team has an opportunity to step up into Performing or slide back into Storming. In the article, "Learn and Grow: How teamwork makes the dream work," on the *your.yale.edu* website, the author explains:

> *Troubled teams have challenges with negative behaviors, lack of trust, low productivity, misalignment, and lack of vision and purpose. However, the sheer definition of team becomes its own solution.*[3]

To accomplish this, project leadership needs to foster a healthy project culture that gets results, regardless of the greater workplace culture that is swirling all around them.

PERFORMING – NOW WE'RE FLYING!

WOOT! This is when the team is working well together, trusting one another, leaning on each other, and maybe even having a little fun while they get project work done.

I mentioned that if you only have two times to spend budget on travel and togetherness, one should be in the beginning. The other one is during the point that feels like the "crescendo" and when in-person time is most valuable to assist with rapid turnaround, clear communication, and ensuring alignment as the team is working hard to deliver the final product, service, or result. This is the final push, the intense period when everything needs to come together successfully, or the project will be deemed a failure.

For example, in software projects, this tends to be during User Acceptance Testing (UAT), which is when the people who will ultimately use the software (or a representative sample of them) get hands-on time with a working version of it. They are often given scenarios to follow, and just like before buying a car, give the software a test drive and put it through its paces. We expect they will ask questions, scrunch their noses, find issues, raise concerns, make brand new requests, and hopefully praise at least one little thing about the solution they've been waiting for and that the team has been working hard to deliver for them.

While the users are testing, the person leading the UAT experience is collecting a list of potential items the team may need to address, noting where the training materials will need to be improved, and running back to the team with this intel. The team needs to rapidly figure out how much effort it will take to resolve the items, and for high priority quick fixes, start resolving them immediately.

During this intense experience, some of the software developers struggle to check their emotions when they want to defend their work. When a lot of items are found, prioritization needs to occur based on business value vs. effort to resolve, and a negotiation tends to ensue. Frankly, UAT can be brutal. However, an in-person experience helps to create an environment where we are all in this together and there is no "us" vs. "them." Ultimately, we all want the same thing, which is the best darn software that addresses the user's needs that we can produce in the time we have. If the project budget allows, it's even better if you can extend the team's time together from UAT through the software launch and into "hypercare" when we make sure that the software is functioning as expected in the production environment.

For a rowing team, this is when they feel like everyone is trying their best and is "in it to win it." Team members are genuinely helpful, motivating, and supportive of each other. They often also feel a positive sense of belonging. However, if they never truly get there and instead are a bunch of individual egomaniacs, then they are in for a really bumpy ride and are probably going to capsize. This results in everyone being cold, wet, and upset, and even more grumbly. It also presents a clear moment for learning and hopefully, turning the proverbial ship around (though if you're on the rowing team, you'll likely want to keep your boat going full speed ahead!).

ADJOURNING/MOURNING – SEE YA! OR A TAD SAD

Just as it sounds, this happens any time a team member leaves the team, and at the end of the project. The project manager can help to prepare the team and ease them through the break-up that's bound to happen. If the project is hard, people practically skip out of the office singing with glee as they adjourn. When the project is a great experience, there can also be some mourning. I certainly have made some great friends after working closely with them on projects, and while proud of our project accomplishments, I was a bit sad to have to go our separate ways toward our next projects.

Have you ever had a relationship that just sort of faded away? Oftentimes in these instances, at least one of the parties is feeling unsettled and wishing for a feeling of closure. Humans need closure. A proper closure meeting followed by a celebration, hosted by the project sponsor and project manager, is highly recommended. If you're a team member, please make the time to actively participate. If not for yourself, for your team. This event, even if it is short, virtual, and with little or no budget, can make a real, positive difference in the hearts and minds of team members.

For a rowing team, Adjourning/Mourning naturally happens at the end of the season, after some wins, some challenges having been overcome, and maybe even some tough losses. Regardless, a celebration and appreciative acknowledgement of everyone's contribution is in order. If the team was particularly tight, there could certainly be some mixed emotions as people disband and settle into the offseason.

ARE WE HAVING FUN YET?

I joined a global company after what must have been an epic leadership retreat, because I heard about it many times from a variety of attendees. It had really hit home with them. When sharing the idea for this chapter with him, my former colleague shared his recollection of the event.

The corporate psychologist ran a team exercise called "Red Chip, Blue Chip" where the theme was "Win as much as you can." People were split into teams working for "Chips Incorporated," and the house would dole out red or blue chips, with blue chips having the most value. The teams were competing intensely against one another, negotiating and trading. In the end, even though one team gathered more blue chips than any other team, it was the house that won! Everyone lost! It was because they were so busy playing against one another, they didn't realize if they had pooled their resources together, they would've beaten the house! The hint was in the beginning. "You all work for Chips Incorporated."

Likely, the reason my colleagues referenced it many times was because there were numerous unfortunate situations where people were working against each other rather than together. I recall many moments where I whined to myself, "But we're all supposed to be on the same team!"

The beautiful thing about Projectland, is that you really can create team spirit amongst your players and accomplish more than you could ever do alone.

CONCLUSION

While many of us were taught to check our emotions at the door before we walk into the office, the reality is that Projectland is intense, and the human element must be considered. A group of people who have likely never worked on this particular thing together, or in this environment, need to figure out how to cooperate in what often amounts to a pressure cooker, with the clock ticking while sitting under management's microscope. Simply realizing that the teaming process is real can be a big step in providing the team with the support they desire and deserve.

Key points to keep in mind:

- Every time a person enters or exits, you start over
- Storming is NORMAL
- Make your goal to get the team up to Performing as quickly as possible.
- Humans need closure!

WHAT'S NEXT?

Now that you have identified all the key players in your version of Projectland and are aware of the teaming process—you need to be sure they are all in your project boat, in the right seats, and ready to row in the right direction. In the next chapter, we'll review a simple, practical secret weapon to make that happen.

PRACTICAL PROJECTAND CHALLENGE

How will you apply what you've learned in your world?
Take Action!

1. If your team is in storming mode, remember it's NORMAL for things to be a little chaotic at the beginning of the process. Use your communication and leadership skills to help them through it.
2. Be aware that when adding or removing new team members, the team goes through the whole process again.
3. Make time for team building (get creative!). The project kick-off and planning work is a great opportunity for collaboration, teamwork, and commitment-building.
4. If you have a virtual team, determine if, how, and when you can get the team together in person for the highest benefit to

the project, while keeping the human element in mind. Include travel and expenses into the project budget. If you must rely on Zoom or some other virtual meeting tool, encourage people to put their cameras on to give a better sense of "being in this together."

5. Because projects end, the team also goes through an adjourning process. If the project is great, don't be surprised if there are mixed emotions and a little mourning too! Consider what you can do to plan to help the team through it and achieve closure. A proper closure meeting followed by a celebration (in person or virtual), hosted by the project sponsor and project manager, is highly recommended.

CHAPTER 13

YOUR SECRET WEAPON TO GET THE PLAYERS ROWING IN THE SAME DIRECTION

"Coaches who can outline plays on a blackboard are a dime a dozen.
The ones who win get inside their players and motivate."[1]
- Vince Lombardi, National Football League
Hall of Fame Coach[2]

S itting at my desk in Philadelphia, I stared anxiously at the clock ticking toward the time the new top boss of the company had promised to call me. I had no idea what it was about. It was either something good or very much not good. My office phone rang at exactly the expected time, so I figured it was him. I took a deep breath and tried to paste a smile on my face, because I heard somewhere that the listener can tell if you're smiling or not.

"Hello, this is Dawn."

"Hi, it's Didier. How are you today?"

"I'm fine, thanks. And you?" *Geez, do I sound as nervous as I feel?*

"I am well," he said in his lovely accent. "I am calling because I'd like to ask if you would be willing to help me. I heard that you ran the PMO here, and that you would be the best choice to help me transform and transition the IT organization from what it was into what it will be under the new entity. It's complicated, with a lot of workstreams, and obviously very sensitive."

Ah, so I'm not getting fired. I sighed with relief and the realization that I'd been holding my breath. As he spoke with me, he was respectful and seemed genuine. I suspected I could learn a lot from him. He was just the type of leader I like to work with. I thanked him for the opportunity, for his faith in me, and agreed to do the job.

As I put down the receiver, I looked at the clock again. He had convinced me to stay on and run one of the most emotionally difficult projects of my career to date. I was impressed and somehow energized to do the best job I could for him and my colleagues, who were feeling extremely confused, shocked, and stressed by the surprise takeover situation. And he accomplished all of that in an eight-minute, audio-only phone call.

IT'S YOUR TURN. LET'S DO THIS!

As this chapter's opening personal story and quote by Vince Lombardi, who is considered to be one of the greatest NFL coaches of all time, suggest, it's not enough to simply show the team the map and tell them what to do. At the start of the project, project leadership has the opportunity to help the team connect their work to the vision, mission, and/or strategy of the organization, help them understand the importance of the project in the context of an inspiring bigger picture, acknowledge them as especially chosen for this important work, and motivate them to do their best to achieve the project goals.

Now it's your turn. Whether you are part of the project leadership team or a team member, you have an important role to play to get this project started smartly and moving in the right direction.

If you've been following the steps outlined in this book, you now have an approved project, all the key players have been successfully recruited, and you're aware of the teaming process. The next step is to bring the team together and welcome them into your project boat, introduce them to each other, show them their seats, point to the goal, and get them ready to row in the right direction.

YOUR SECRET WEAPON AT THE START: THE KICKOFF MEETING

Ok, maybe it's not much of a secret, but the kickoff meeting itself is an important and powerful tool. Please don't skip over this in the name of speed. If you do, it'll be sure to backfire. In this section, we'll talk about how to prepare for a solid, succinct kickoff with all the key players.

First, what is a kickoff meeting anyway? The term originates from football, and in Projectland it's generally the first official gathering of the full project team. This meeting comes after the project has been approved, the high-level project information has been defined and agreed upon by leadership, and before detailed planning begins. The purpose is to create alignment between everyone involved with the project, explain their roles, and set the stage for them to be successful working together to create the project's product, service, or result.

The kickoff clearly indicates the official start of a journey that no one has gone on before with these people, at this time, and/or in this place.

If you are the project manager in charge of organizing the kickoff meeting, I suggest you work on scheduling it as soon as possible, even if you don't have the materials ready yet. This is because it is often very difficult to find an available time window for a group of people to get together in the short term. You likely will not be able to find a time that works for everyone until the following week or the week after anyway. Do include the kickoff meeting objectives and topics in the calendar invitation and indicate your excitement to get everyone together to kick off the project. Then, schedule a prep meeting with your sponsor and work on the draft kickoff deck that you can review together.

If you work for a service organization (e.g., a consulting firm, a financial services company, etc.), and you've been hired by a client, then you will likely have an internal kickoff meeting that will prepare your team to have a kickoff meeting with the client next. This extra step can help ensure that your team looks like a cohesive group and a well-oiled machine to the client who is investing in you, and who wants to be reassured that they've made the right decision in hiring your organization. For instance, if your team members ask questions that the client believes they should already know the answers to, you will not look professional or prepared. Poor performance at the kickoff can result in an immediate vote of no confidence, and dismissal. So, don't mess this up. Over-prepare, if necessary, to be sure everyone on your team is up to speed and ready to bring their A-game to the client.

What if Everyone Isn't Available for the Kickoff?

The ideal situation is when everyone is available for the kickoff meeting. However, sometimes this isn't possible, particularly for very large teams. Someone is bound to be out of the office on vacation, furiously wrapping up another project, or ill. If you are working to schedule the meeting and are able to see everyone's calendars, find a time when most people are available. If just a few people show as busy, ask the busy bees if it would be possible for them to change the appointment on their calendar so they can join.

If it's not possible to schedule everyone at the preferred time, you can push ahead and record it, following up with any missing people later. Or you can delay the start. The decision is up to the sponsor.

However, if Sponsor Shirley is the missing person, it's best if she can at least kick-off the project for the first several minutes. She should apologize for not being able to stay for the entire meeting, reassuring everyone that she worked together with Project Manager Pierre to prepare the kickoff materials. She can emphasize that she has full confidence in him to lead the remainder of the meeting solo and looks forward to debriefing with him upon returning.

This is best done by the sponsor live, but if required due to the urgency of the meeting, a video recording will do. Preparing the video is in addition to everything else she needs to explain at the start. If the sponsor does not do the apologizing, explaining that the reason for the absence is unavoidable, then she will appear to not fully support or be personally committed to the project. That sends the absolute wrong message to the team and sets the wrong tone before the project has even started. Team members tend to ask themselves why they should be 110% committed if the top leader on the project isn't. Particularly for team members who know that lack of management support is a key reason projects fail, it is fair for them to be skeptical.

Next, I'll share two kickoff scenarios:

- The 1-hour(ish) kickoff meeting, and
- The multi-day kickoff and detailed planning experience, which begins with the 1-hour(ish) kickoff meeting.

THE ONE-HOUR(ISH) PROJECT KICKOFF MEETING

At this point, each team member should be clear on what role they will play on the project, as well as be assured their boss has approved the time for them to work on it. If they have questions about the priority of the project versus other responsibilities, their boss should have helped make that clear to them. Otherwise, the project manager's assumption is that they will be available per the project schedule.

Who should participate?

Everyone named so far as a team member should participate. This includes the sponsor, steering team, and team leads if you have them, and the "subject matter expert" team members as well. This does *not* typically include any stakeholders who are outside these project team roles. Oftentimes, if you need to make stakeholders aware that the project has begun along with a few key details, that can be done with a brief communication (e.g., email). The kickoff meeting is for the team. Organizations that are very inclusive may feel uncomfortable with "excluding" people. This is Projectland. It's different here. There are different rules. The project leadership team needs to set the tone at the beginning, that the project team needs to focus, and anyone outside the project team who needs to be consulted or informed, will be. A key principle is to be respectful of everyone's time, and that includes stakeholders.

What should be included in the kickoff meeting invitation?

If there is an approved business case, project charter, cost justification, statement of work, or other official documents that collectively spell out what is expected, the kickoff meeting invitation should include them. The invitation should request that attendees read them prior to the meeting and come prepared with their questions in order to keep the meeting to one hour. It should also include the objectives and a list of topics for the meeting. More on this next. It's even better if it contains the agenda (including expected timings), though for a one-hour meeting, including the timings isn't as critical. In the example invitation available on the Project Guru Press website (projectguru-press.com/meettheplayers/tools), you will see timing ranges are included. This demonstrates a nice professional touch, without being overly rigid and intimidating.

How long should it take to prepare and how much warning should people have?

Here's how the timing often plays out, where K stands for kickoff.

K-minus 1-2 weeks – The project manager or sponsor's admin schedules the meeting when most people are available. Those who aren't available are asked to move their calendars around. The full team receives a meeting notice once the sponsor agrees to the day, time, and attendance expectations (e.g., who can/can't attend, whether it will be recorded for those who cannot attend, and which formats are acceptable – in-person, hybrid, or fully remote). As noted above, the meeting request includes the objectives, agenda, and project approval documents (e.g., business case) with a respectful request that attendees review it and prepare their questions to keep the meeting to one hour.

Attendees should look at their calendars and be sure to set aside time to do so.

K-minus at least 48 Hours – To be sure there is enough time to fully prepare, the project manager and sponsor should plan to meet to finalize the kickoff deck, talking points, handoffs, and logistics, at least 48 hours prior to the kickoff meeting. Beyond the deck details, they need to align on how they, too, will look like a professional and prepared leadership duo at the kickoff. For instance:

- Project Manager Pierre will set up the room early and have the deck ready.
- Sponsor Shirley will aim to join five minutes prior to the meeting to greet team members as they arrive.
- Shirley kicks off the meeting with opening remarks, including the *why* behind the project, and then turns it over to Pierre.
- Pierre walks through the details with the team and then turns it back over to Shirley at the end for closing remarks.

If the kickoff meeting includes a lot of team members and is virtual or hybrid, they may need to determine other logistics, such as:

- How they'll watch the chat for questions
- Whether they'll ask people to save their questions to the end or take them along the way
- How they'll capture and distribute notes
- What they'll do if someone tries to take the meeting sideways.

A little bit of what may feel like "over preparation" is worth it to set the tone appropriately. Team members need to trust that they're getting on a boat that isn't doomed to sink.

What are typical objectives and topics covered in a kickoff meeting?

If you are the project manager, I highly recommend that you grab the *High-Level Project Kickoff Thinking Tool* at the Project Guru Press website (project-gurupress.com / meettheplayers / tools), which contains all the information included here in a PowerPoint format that you can use as a starting point framework to draft the kickoff experience. Then you can review it with your sponsor. If you're not the project manager, keep reading! It's nice to know what to expect, and if any of these areas don't get covered by the project manager or sponsor, you'll know what questions to ask.

The typical objectives for the Kickoff meeting are:

- To kick off our project
- To ensure everyone knows their roles and our high-level plan
- To determine our cadence in working as a team

After the opening remarks, the project manager will typically review the high-level plan, including:

- Background, to be sure "why this project is important now" is clear to everyone; this may have been covered in the opening remarks by the sponsor
- Objectives – what success looks like and what "done" means
- High-level schedule and key milestones – this is the "when"
- Scope – in / out and key deliverables – this is the "what"
- Top risks and responses – these tend to address the top concerns and any "elephants in the room" that team members may be worried about
- Cost / effort estimates – If the budget (effort and / or investment) vs. the value is important to note, include it. For instance, if you want the team to know that the budget is $20 Million, and the executive team expects a $100 Million minimum return in 3 years to deem the project a success, say so. Otherwise, the cost element is often removed for the full team, particularly in organizations that are sensitive to sharing the project budget / anticipated investment) or for projects that are fully internal-effort based.

- Assumptions and Constraints – Again assumptions are things we think are true but there is no proof (e.g., resources will be available per the schedule), and constraints are things that are limiting your options (e.g., full team meetings will need to be held at 8 AM Eastern to accommodate the global team).
- Initial project organization – The initial project organization is a picture of the project team that looks like an organizational chart (see Chapter 4, Figure 4.1 "Typical Projectland Reporting Structure"). It shows the project sponsor at the top and acknowledges key stakeholders outside of the project team as well. Everyone at the kickoff should see their name on the chart. In spots where we don't know who will be assigned yet, we have the role definition like "Bobcat Operator," and we specify "To Be Determined (TBD)" as a placeholder in the name area.
- RACI – This is a grid that defines the high-level activities on the left column and the roles across top. It is meant to clarify decision and engagement expectations for each major role group on the project. The project manager may present this as a draft for review and feedback by the team, to acknowledge that the draft might be wrong, gather input, and gain team buy-in. For each activity row, under each role column, there is an assignment corresponding to the RACI acronym, as follows.

Responsible – These are the do-ers and there can be more than one per activity

Accountable – There can be only one accountable role per activity. The best way to remember this is that there can only be one "A" per line, because that person's "A" is on the line. (Sorry, HR friends, but I bet you'll never forget this one rule now!)

Consult – These roles are consulted before a decision is made.

Inform – These roles are informed after a decision is

made. If someone feels they should be consulted before a decision is made, and they are merely informed, they can get upset. This is one key reason that setting expectations using this RACI tool in the beginning can be so helpful. It could look as simple as Figure 13.1 below:

ID	Major Activities	Sponsor	Steering Team	Project Manager	Project Team	Team Lead	Customer Rep	Enter Add'l Role
1	Project Leadership	**A**	R	R	I	C	C	
2	Project Plans	C	I	**A**	C	R	C	
3	Product Deliverable Creation	I	I	C	R	**A**	C	
4	Product Deliverable Sign-off	C	I	R	I	R	**A**	

Figure 13.1 - Sample RACI Chart

- Final feedback / Q&A / Next Steps – This topic allows for final input, questions, and clarification on immediate next steps. For instance, a key item to determine with the team, in alignment with the defined meeting objectives, is deciding the cadence in working as a team. For instance, the project manager may ask what days and times work best for a recurring team meeting. Another next step could be that the project manager will be following up with those who were unable to attend.
- Closing Remarks – Finally, if still in attendance at the end, the sponsor may offer closing, encouraging remarks, and thank everyone for joining. If not, the project manager should do this, and may emphasize key points from the sponsor's opening remarks.

If the project leadership team is not ready to cover one or more of these topics, it may be because they have not yet had the chance to plan them and they are looking for the team to do so as a group. That's fine too. You only know what you know in the beginning, and you have to figure out the rest. Even if you do have all of these topics covered at the high-level, there are often more questions than answers at the start. Don't be surprised if the details are not worked out yet. In fact, more detailed planning is often what happens next. How we handle that is covered in the next chapter.

K plus 24 Hours or Less – As soon as possible, but no more than twenty-four hours from the start of the kick-off meeting, the project manager should send a written follow-up to all attendees including an uneditable version of the meeting output (e.g., PDF), key points, a big thank you to those in attendance, a request for those who did not attend to review the recording, and an invitation to answer any questions they may have. A brief reminder of agreed-upon next steps can also be helpful.

CONCLUSION

In this chapter, you learned about how project pros create a simple and powerful clear project start via a one-hour(ish) kickoff meeting. This sets the stage for developing the "no excuses, everything is figure-outable together" mindset needed for winning teams. Your team is now aware of the project's goals and mission and everyone's roles in the effort. Plus, your sponsor has demonstrated visible support. The team is now in the project boat together, knows where their seat is, and is poised to grab their oars and start rowing in the same direction.

Some projects are simple, and the team knows just what to do next. However, in the case of larger, very pioneering, or more complex projects, you may need to add time for more detailed, immersive planning, to help the team figure out how they will get from where they are to where the sponsor expects them to go. Otherwise, they feel like they are sitting in a little project boat, gripping the dock for dear life, because while they've been told to start moving in the right direction, all they see is fog and shadows that could be sea monsters.

WHAT'S NEXT?

In the next chapter, we'll cover what an efficient version of detailed, immersive planning can look and feel like when we walk through the *Multi-day Project Kickoff and Detailed Planning Experience*. This will help lift the "now-what-do-we-do" fog, so that the team feels confident in pushing off the dock.

Plus, if your organization doesn't already value planning as important, keep reading! Planning is doing, and doing planning can make all the difference to figuring out the best, most efficient way to reach your project's goals.

PRACTICAL PROJECTLAND CHALLENGE

What actions can you take to apply the lessons in this chapter to get your project formally started on the right foot?

Take Action!

1. Plan or prepare to attend a kickoff meeting with all of the players who are defined so far. If you're the project manager, download the *High-Level Project Kickoff Thinking Tool* (PowerPoint) to help you from the Project Guru Press website (projectgurupress.com/meettheplayers/tools).
2. Put your best foot forward. Remember, the team is at the Forming stage here, so you can do your part to help team members feel welcome and valued. Prepare to set the right tone. Own your expertise and your role, while being humble. Communicate your own version of, "I look forward to working with and learning from all of you." Whether you're the new intern and it's your first job ever, or an experienced expert, you can say that and mean it.
3. If you're asked to introduce yourself at the kickoff meeting, plan to be brief. The clock is ticking.

4. If you're asked to review a pre-read and prepare your questions prior to the meeting, please make time to do so. Project leaders can always tell who is prepared, and this is part of being a good team member. Often, projects are a great way to get yourself noticed by leaders you wouldn't normally interact with, so it is in your best interest to make a good first impression.

5. Assess whether the one-hour(ish) kickoff meeting is enough or if you need a more detailed, multi-day experience. You may need to read the next chapter first to decide.

CHAPTER 14
YOUR SECRET WEAPON PART TWO: WHEN PART ONE JUST ISN'T ENOUGH

"You were born to win, but to be a winner, you must plan to win,
prepare to win, and expect to win."
- Zig Ziglar, Author and Motivational Speaker

"Dawn, do you have a minute? I really want to show you something," says the very excited client project manager.

"Sure," I reply, "I have a whole 5 minutes before my next meeting." *How could I deny him? I'm so curious to know what on earth is so exciting!*

He quickly leads me to a conference room, and a few other people sense what's happening and start to tag along. The energy is so electric, that I have this feeling like we're about to start dancing down the hall as if we're in a musical. He opens the door, and I walk in behind him. Making a voila motion with his hand, he proudly shows me the walls, while nodding to the others who joined us. Everyone is beaming. He says, "I thought you might like to see that we took your training to heart." The whole wall is filled with large, colorful Post-It® notes. He continues, "It was a great experience... for all of us."

No one, but perhaps a 3M sales executive who needed to make his quota, could have been more thrilled.

WHEN THE FIRST SECRET WEAPON JUST ISN'T ENOUGH TO GET THE TEAM TO PUSH OFF THE DOCK AND START ROWING

In the previous chapter, we explored the one-hour(ish) kickoff meeting, with opening remarks by the project sponsor and a walkthrough of the high-level details by the project manager. It's a great start and often all that's needed to kick things off. But for bigger, hairier, and scarier projects, you may need something more. You may need what I fondly refer to as:

THE MULTI-DAY PROJECT KICKOFF & DETAILED PLANNING EXPERIENCE

This is a detailed planning experience to engage the team in taking the high-level plans presented and explained in the kickoff meeting down to the next level of detail.

Who should participate?

A key tenet to keep in mind at this point and throughout the project is that your sponsor and steering team, if you have one, should *stay out of the sausage-making*. The project manager leads the team to create the sausage for the leadership team to taste-test, provide feedback on, taste-test a final time, and then provide final approval of the recipe along with a genuine message of, "Well done, team."

This "stay out of the sausage-making" tenet is for the benefit of both the subject-matter-expert team members and the leadership team. Since this is the first time in the history of the world this team is creating this particular brand of sausage, the process tends to get messy. The team needs to begin to trust each other, ask questions that might be silly, try things, iterate, and be wrong. Often, team members don't feel that they're subject matter experts yet, and are nervous about offering their ideas in front of leaders. Because of this, you may not get the full participation that you need with leadership in the room. On the flip side, leadership team members tend to be hard to schedule for large blocks of time, many do not have any tolerance for the minutia required, and even if they do, their time is better spent leading than mucking around in the weeds. This is the principle that the following suggested experience design is based on.

That said, many new sponsors are reluctant to NOT be involved in the sausage-making. If that is the case, explain the above concerns to them, share the below suggested alternative plan with them, and if they still insist on being part of the sausage-making experience, then fine. You did your best to warn them that it could backfire.

When is it appropriate for them to join? In two instances. One is if they are the main subject matter expert of a particular part of the project. For that piece, they are really acting as a team member, and should work with the project manager to plan the details of that part. For the rest of the project parts, it is often fine for them to exit. The second instance is for the high-level review of the plan in their sponsor role as the accountable person for the project.

I mentioned it above, but it bears repeating for clarity. Stakeholders are outside of the immediate project team and are NOT included in the team's kickoff event, nor are they needed for more detailed planning work. In fact, part of the planning work will be to identify who they are, as well as how and when to communicate with them. It is usually far too early to worry about stakeholder communications now.

Keep in mind, the people who participate the most in the detailed planning experience are the team leads, at minimum, and any identified subject matter experts, all led by the project manager. The sponsor is brought in for the first taste-test and gives feedback. When the sponsor is satisfied (often after several iterations), if there is a steering team, the sponsor may ask the project manager and team leads to present a "next-level-down" plan to them. Generally, this is curated at the appropriate level of detail. You do not want to include information so far down in the weeds that the steering team will lose their minds. This review is particularly important if the team has discovered some differences between what is possible, and the expectations set in the kickoff. If inquisitive steering team members wish to dive deeper, the appropriate players can follow up with them after the meeting.

Here's what a multi-day kickoff and detailed planning experience could look like. First, it is best if the same conference room can be booked for the entire experience to reduce confusion and commute-time for team members.

FULL TEAM KICKOFF (DAY 1)

Start with the one-hour(ish) kickoff meeting with the full team (as described in the previous chapter). If this meeting is hosted in person or a virtual/in-person hybrid, bring in food for those folks who are in the room. This sets the tone that the team is special and appreciated.

If the multi-day experience is planned, the actual agenda for the next few days of detailed planning will be one of the items to cover under the "next steps" topic at the end of the project kickoff meeting, to be sure everyone knows when they're needed and what to expect. In general, one term I like for explaining what comes next is "walk the walls." Because that is exactly what the next exercise feels like—a showcase for a wall display of Post-It notes that the sponsor will later review. The project manager and team leaders will start filling up walls with Post-It notes representing high-level deliverables, and since the sponsor is often "driven up the wall" with this level of sausage-making, you will make it clear when you expect to bring them in for their walk-throughs (i.e., the taste test / feedback sessions described above). The reason Post-It notes are suggested is because planning is best done in the beginning as a collaborative exercise, not an individual thinking exercise done in isolation.

At the end of the one-hour(ish) kickoff meeting, the sponsor and steering team will continue with their day, and the team will dive into the detailed planning exercises outlined below.

INITIAL "REVOLVING DOOR" WBS PLANNING WITH TEAM LEADS (DAY 1 POST-KICKOFF THROUGH THE MORNING OF DAY 2)

What is WBS Planning?

A lot of sponsors want to know how long the project will take and how much it will cost. And the answer from team members is often, "I don't know," along with an extreme level of anxiousness around giving leadership any answer whatsoever. This is normal. The reason it's normal is that often, the team doesn't feel it has enough information about what *it* is. They can't tell the leadership team how much time *it* will take or how much *it* will cost if they aren't clear on what *it* is they are expected to deliver. Fair, right?

The Work Breakdown Structure (WBS) defines the *it* at a detailed enough level to get the team clear on what the deliverables are. When approved, the WBS defines the total scope of the project. In essence, the WBS is a hierarchical, noun-based representation of the deliverables that make up the project. My preference is do this visually, using the Post-It notes and arranging them so that it looks like an organizational chart.

If the highest-level deliverable is a wooden chair to sell to customers, the sub-deliverables may be the seat, the back, the legs, the customer assembly instructions, the packaging, as well as marketing deliverables, manufacturing SOPs, contracts with a lumberyard, and so on. Each of these may be broken down by even smaller sub-deliverables until you get to the point where you have a work package that can be handed to one person to deliver in 8 to 80 hours. If it's too big to deliver in two weeks or less, it can usually be broken down further.

The WBS thinking tool is the secret weapon to avoid scope creep later. Once *it* is defined, the team can identify or confirm the resources they need to do deliver *it* and begin to create a realistic, detailed schedule after that, based on dependencies and actual resource availability. This is why I always recommend the team work to build the WBS first thing after the kickoff meeting. It brings clarity to what *it* is and helps everyone align around *it*. The anxiety balloon around not knowing what *it* is that's expected of the team can then start to deflate.

What is the "Revolving Door" Method and Why is it Great?

In many organizations I've worked with, people are spread far too thin across their "day jobs" and projects. Especially in these environments, the "revolving door" method can set the tone that project leadership is being respectful of everyone's time. I find it works very well, particularly for projects with a number of teams or workstreams led by team leads. It gives the opportunity for the project manager and the team lead to begin to establish a respectful, one-on-one working relationship for the project. The project manager can sit in the same room, and based on their availability, have the team leads come in one at a time.

Rather than lock all the team leaders in the room with the project manager all day, the project manager locks themselves in the room, and the team leaders come in one by one. It will feel like there is a revolving door for the project manager, but it is a very efficient way to get a first draft WBS created. This should be pre-arranged on the team leader's calendars to be sure their preferred timeframe is booked. The project manager should remember to schedule break times for themselves in between these one-on-one meetings. This work could take the entire day or more depending on how many team leads there are.

What do these Revolving Door sessions look like?

Without the "Revolving Door" method, the alternative looks like one team lead sitting in the hot seat feeling like everyone is staring at them, while the rest of the team leads wonder why they have to sit there and watch the person squirm and struggle to think in real-time with all that staring going on.

Instead, using the "Revolving Door" method, the project manager is in the reserved room and greets one team leader at a time. The project manager patiently leads each team leader privately through the thinking process.

To get the WBS started, the project manager asks each team lead what "things" they need to deliver as part of the project. If you're doing this exercise in person, it's nice to have Post-It note pads in a variety of different colors and ask the team lead to choose their favorite. This way, they will remember which color is theirs and it will make more sense during the later group planning exercises. When projects get big, it's easier for people to focus on their own colors. This color technique can also be done in many virtual tools (e.g., Trello).

For example, if the overall objective of the project is to create a backyard oasis for the Smith family, then the leadership team would likely consist of the pool construction team leader and landscaping team leader. The pool construction team leader might say his favorite color is blue and that his team needs to deliver a giant hole, electrical, plumbing, and a diving board. The landscaping team leader may say her favorite color is green and explain that her team needs to deliver the draft landscape design blueprint and final approved version, as well as the drop-shipped plants, special soil, mulch, and of course, the final landscaping, per the approved design.

Notice that these are all written as things, and not tasks. Invariably, team leaders will start to talk about what they need to do, and the project manager will ask them, "Okay, but what is the thing?" until the thing is clear. This is the expected deliverable that is tangible and verifiable. What is *not* tangible and verifiable? An "understanding." For instance, in many projects, there is something you want the recipient of your product, service, or result to understand. This is not a thing. What *is* a thing would be something that could aid in someone's understanding, such as a training class, a written job aid checklist, or a help screen.

The other thing to watch out for at this point is to make the thing crystal clear. For instance, if you say that your team will deliver a "report," what does that mean? Is it a 500-page publishable-in-a-medical-journal report or is it a 10ish page PowerPoint report? Clearly the amount of effort and time it will take to deliver the former is much more than the latter, so get as clear as you can in proposing what you think is the skinniest version of the thing that will satisfy the need. Think Jenny Craig, not Fat Bastard[1] here. The skinnier the deliverable, the faster your team can deliver it.

FULL TEAM LEAD DRAFT WBS WALK-THROUGH

Once the project manager has met with all the team leads, they all get back together in the room again. This usually happens at the end of Day 1 or the beginning of Day 2 depending on everyone's availability. If there are a lot of team leads, it can be helpful for the project manager to put all the input together at the end of the day, and then come in the next day ready with a fresh brain to facilitate all the leads. This can certainly be done virtually instead, if necessary.

However, as I mentioned before, if you're going to spend travel money, the beginning is ideal for investing in face-to-face time. Ideas often flow more naturally, easily, and quickly in person and team camaraderie begins and accelerates.

Regardless of when it happens, the goal is for each of the team leads to walk through and explain their deliverables. While there is no timing discussed yet, because we're focused on the scope (i.e., the things), there is usually a logical order that the team lead will take as they walk through the things their team will deliver.

The project manager and team leads need to actively listen to the presenting team leader to understand and look for dependencies, as well as consider what might be missing. For instance, the landscaping team lead may ask at what point the giant pile of dirt made after digging the hole for the pool will be cleared out and who does that? This brings up an important deliverable that may have been missed. If the pool construction crew does this, the project manager will add a Post-It note in blue that says, "giant pile of dirt removed and land-scaping team notified."

This is also an opportunity to scrutinize some of the deliverables and agree on which items are truly needed or which may be redundant with other deliverables being produced by other players. In other words, it's a chance for everyone to see the whole scope of the project and make sure it's as lean as can be, with no redundancies. Everyone should understand why each item is there and why it's important.

It also may require the project manager to facilitate agreements where parties disagree, encouraging everyone to always keep the goals of the organization and the project's customer in mind. In circumstances where they can't agree, the project manager will make a note to review the item with the sponsor and ask for their input during their "taste test" review that comes next.

SPONSOR WBS DRAFT WALK-THROUGH (DAY 2)

Once the team leads are satisfied that they have a good draft of the WBS, they are ready to walk through it with the sponsor. Having already practiced with each other, they should be comfortable doing this.

For a small project, the project manager may do this alone because there are no team leaders, or they may do this with some SMEs present who can speak to the deliverables when there are questions. If there are team leads, it's helpful for the project manager to serve as the facilitator while the team leaders present their parts to the sponsor and one another once again. In the process of explaining their thinking aloud about what they need to deliver to meet the objectives, new ideas and questions they didn't think of earlier will come up.

For any project deliverables that are unclear, the team leads should be prepared to ask clarifying questions about what the sponsor is envisioning, as the answer might impact who does those deliverables and the timeline. (Remember our 10-page PowerPoint or 500-page publishable report example from earlier?) The sponsor may also have questions and insights that can help the team refine the deliverables.

I keep talking about deliverables here because that is all the WBS is. A hierarchal structure that defines the deliverables, which are tangible, verifiable things. Remember, the schedule, the how, and even the exact assignments don't matter yet. This is important to remind everyone when they start to downward spiral into a rabbit hole of details.

How long does this take and when does it happen?

If the project managers and team leaders get through their collective WBS walkthrough during the morning of Day 2, they could likely use a lunch break, and it surely would be nice if lunch is brought in for them. The sponsor could join after the lunch break so that team members are largely done chewing before they present to the top project boss. If it's virtual, don't forget to give your hardworking team leaders a long enough mental and food break so they can do their best. After all, they are still in Forming mode, and often want to make a good impression here.

How do you know when you're done and ready to move on?

At the end of the walkthrough with the sponsor, the sponsor and team should feel good that they have at least 80% of what *it* is that we're delivering defined. You usually know when that "good enough" point is after you've revisited the project objectives and made sure you aren't missing anything important required to deliver them successfully, and when everyone looks at each other and can't really think of anything else. As the facilitator, the project manager will ensure that the questions that can't be answered in the room and require follow-up are clearly documented and assigned.

For instance, the landscaping team leader might need to ask their Italian tile subject matter expert a question about the type of grout they prefer to use for outdoor applications in the client's environment. In the meantime, "TBD Grout" (i.e., To Be Determined) is an acceptable defined deliverable. 80% or better is winning at this point. You don't have to know everything to continue to the next planning exercise. Additionally, when you go through the next part, you may discover more "things" that you missed in the initial WBS. When that happens, as the Bobby McFerrin 1988 song says, "Don't worry, be happy!" It's normal to iterate in the beginning.

CREATING THE INITIAL DETAILED PROJECT SCHEDULE (DAY 3)

The WBS represents the "what," and the project schedule represents the "when." While the team leaders exit to go find the answers to any remaining questions, the project manager can transform the WBS into an initial schedule based on basic logic and the initial high-level timeline presented in the one-hour(ish) kick-off meeting. When the planning workshops are happening in person, this is a matter of arranging the Post-It notes from the WBS wall along a timeline on another wall. When the planning workshops are conducted virtually, this is done by copying the WBS into another file and moving the deliverables into a timeline view. This can often be done at the end of Day 2, so that it's ready for the team leaders to come back in and review fresh on Day 3.

Some folks at this point ask if they really need to lock everyone into "so much time" for dedicated planning workshops when everyone is busy. While this exercise can be accomplished across weeks, it is best to schedule it on contiguous days for both speed and ease of remembering. The longer the time in between sessions, the higher the risk that participants will not remember what they meant and miss something important. Particularly for projects where speed is a high priority, extending the planning workshops extends the timeline of the entire project. Front-loading team time togetherness also helps you accelerate the teaming process explained in the previous chapter.

When the team leaders come into the room, whether real or virtual, they will be looking at all of the deliverables they defined, moved into a schedule format. Many times, this means there are months or weeks across the top of the wall or virtual board, and the project manager did the best job possible at laying things out in logical order. Again, this is simply for efficient use of the team leaders' time. But also, by doing this work, the project manager begins to understand how the pieces might fit together, which is an important part of their role. If this feels impossible, the project manager can employ the same "revolving door" strategy here, asking each of the team leads to come in and help them place their pieces on the schedule. Then once again, you need to get everyone together to see the full picture and align around it.

When I've done this or coached project managers who are creating the initial schedule, the recommended opening statement to the group of team leads is something like, "I did my best, but I know this is wrong. It's our job next to also do our best to make it as right as we can, based on what makes sense to us. Then, we'll bring in the sponsor and 'walk the walls' with them again." Then, the project manager walks through the schedule while the team leaders sit back and think, ask questions, and suggest where to move things around. Sometimes they get really excited, jump up, and start moving things around themselves. That's great!

When they are done, they should have a solid initial schedule and questions to be clarified. The team leaders also need to see what they can do to explain any differences from the high-level schedule presented at the kick-off meeting on Day 1 and emphasize where there is alignment, because the sponsor will want to know, "Can we still make the initial goal or not? And if not, why not?" If the team has laid the schedule out and the expectation is that the sponsor is going to be grossly disappointed in the timeline, then preparing an alternative version to show "what we *can* deliver in the timeframe you hoped," is smart.

You may wish to plan on having your sponsor ready to come in mid-afternoon on Day 3, so that you have at least two hours to walk the walls together. In this case, the project manager likely will stand to facilitate the walk-through while pointing to the deliverables on the wall timeline, and the team leaders will chime in with clarifications. The sponsor should again seek to understand and provide helpful advice and guidance.

This leadership team should also take another look at "month one." How realistic is it that everything proposed can actually get done in the first month given other commitments underway? Do the team leaders have everything they need and are they approved to get their team members working on these deliverables?

At the end of Day 3, the participating leadership team (i.e., the sponsor, project manager, and team leads) should feel good that they have defined the majority of the key things that they will deliver, as well as when they will deliver them. There should be a clear list of questions to answer, along with who will answer them and when this group will get back together to review the answers. Everyone should feel good about the initial plans and know what work has been approved for their teams to get started with confidence. If there is a steering team, the leadership team should also plan on when the first official steering team meeting will be and what the story is that they want to tell in that meeting. This way, if any of the steering team members ask any of them questions about progress and next steps, they will know what their collective answer is.

CONCLUSION

Whether you've completed only a one-hour(ish) kickoff meeting or a multi-day kickoff and detailed planning experience, you should feel good that the team is clear on their roles and feel confident enough to push off the dock. While you won't have all the answers, the team should be ready to row in the direction of the project's objectives.

If they are new to working together in Projectland and completed the recommended group detailed planning experience, then they should also have started the process of *forming* as a project team.

WHAT'S NEXT?

WOW! You're almost at the end of the book and off to the races with your project! Keep reading to learn what the wild world of racing has to do with succeeding in Projectland.

PRACTICAL PROJECTLAND CHALLENGE

What will you do with what you've learned?
Take Action!

1. Consider the best way to work with your team to take the high-level plan to the next level of detail. Is a multi-day planning experience possible? If so, can you get everyone together in person? If not, what is the next best thing you can do to keep the positive forward momentum going post-kickoff?
2. If you're the project manager, download the *Top 10 Tips for leading a WBS Planning session* from the Project Guru Press website (projectgurupress.com/meettheplayers/tools).

3. If you're the sponsor, self-assess. What can you do in the beginning to help your team feel empowered? One way is to stay out of the sausage-making. If this is uncomfortable for you, why? What might make it ok? Remember, how you lead in the beginning, sets the stage for the entire project.

4. If you're a steering team member, self-assess. What can you do to ensure that the steering team is properly engaged at the right moments to make sure that the team is steadily making progress toward the objectives and poised to deliver the expected business value? When steering team meetings are set, be sure to block time on your calendar to prepare and follow-up on any actions, if needed.

5. If you're a team lead and/or SME, what pre-thinking or research can you do to bring your A-game to the planning work? Resist diving into the work before you have buy-in, so that you don't waste your precious talent and time on the wrong things. Remember, leading by example can help you shine and inspire the team.

CHAPTER 15
YOU'RE OFF TO THE RACES!

"If everything seems under control, you're not going fast enough."
- Mario Andretti, Driver of the Century[1]

"Who's meeting is this?" questioned the man sitting at the head of the conference table, who had just successfully completed a $300 Million bet-the-company global SAP implementation. As I was the lowest ranking consultant in the room, sitting next to my boss, who had already retired from IBM, and our account manager, who had been working this and other Fortune 500 accounts for many years, I kept my mouth shut while silently thinking: *I'm pretty sure it's your meeting, so this just got a little weird and we didn't even start yet.*

Fortunately, the awkward moment was soon cut off when the door opened in a hurry and a petite woman with strong "boss lady" vibes flew into the room. There were no seats left at the table. Several men started to scramble in an effort to offer her a place to sit. She essentially shushed them and said, "No need. I'm only going to be a moment." She nodded at the man at the head of the table and said, "Ralph, this is your meeting," then she turned to look at my colleagues and I while I gulped.

"Everyone," she said, "I asked for you to come here, because we have a problem and I do believe that you can help us. Frankly, I was disappointed and embarrassed to have had to call engineering to get a project manager like Ralph for the SAP project, because when we looked around IT, there was no one we could trust to do the job well. We need to create a strong project management capability in IT. I asked Ralph to lead the effort. Thanks for coming. I'll leave you all to it." She nodded and left the room.

Ralph looked at all of us, and said, "It's true. I'm from engineering. I spent my entire career over there, managing projects to build chemical plants and whatnot around the world, until she called." Then he smirked. "I still don't even know how to spell SAP." We all laughed. He'd broken the heaviness in the room with a little self-deprecating humor. I thought, "I really hope we get to work with him. I know I'd learn a lot." And I did.

One of my favorite Ralphisms came from his love of car racing. He used to say, "Like racing, in order to go fast, you have to know when to go slow."

Once, Ralph took me to a go-kart track. He had been competitively racing, and I happened to tell him the story about when I had taken my younger brother go-kart racing. "It was definitely fun," I explained, "until I almost lost my toes." The track manager said I would have left a little lighter if it hadn't been for the Dr. Martens shoes I was wearing. All because some angry guy wasn't terribly pleased that I was remaining ahead of him, so he spun me out and landed on top of me, with his kart grazing my shoe hard enough to leave a black skid mark. Ralph's reply to this was a serious question, "Would you like to learn how to race, so that doesn't happen again?" I did. I really did.

We got to the racetrack, and he must have been a VIP there, because before I knew it, we were in a conference room with a whiteboard. He drew the track in black marker. He then drew the cart paths in red marker. He pointed to where to go slow and where to go fast. "You go fast on the straightaways, and then you slow down on the curve and position yourself to go faster on the next straightaway." That day, I really understood better what he'd meant by his paradoxical wisdom. Plus, I had fun and didn't even come close to losing any toes.

In projects, a definite time that you need to go slow in order to go fast later is at the beginning. When a project lands on your lap, you know that jumping up and starting to run immediately in some direction, any direction, so that you look busy, is not your best response. Rather, you know that it's time to be thoughtful; to be sure that you're clear on the problem to solve or the opportunity to seize; to work with some smart folks and figure out the best, smartest way to reach the goal.

You now know that it's the people who will make or break your success in Projectland. You know that every project is unknown territory, and anything can happen. Since most projects fail, and a lack of management support is one top reason for failure, you know that identifying the right leadership players who will lead the team through the wilderness safely, is key. Because if this isn't possible, then perhaps you can simply stop here and shelve the idea until the right leader steps up and makes it a priority.

Once the leadership team is on board, it's time to create your "dream team" of subject matter experts, or at least "love the ones you're with." These are the players who, collectively as a team, have the skills and working styles that are a fit for creating your project's product, service, or result.

After these fine folks have been recruited, a kickoff meeting brings them together to formally mark the start of the project. Since all projects by definition have a beginning, this event helps everyone to mark the start, look around the table at the players, assess where they fit, and learn what to expect from everyone else.

Whether conducted as an add-on to the kick-off or over the course of several weeks, more detailed planning is next. Planning together does so much more than create the plan. It aligns everyone around "what we're doing exactly" (the scope), "when we're doing it" (the schedule), and at least at the team level, "who is doing it" (the resources). The process of creating the plan creates buy-in, provides the opportunity to form as a team early, and solidifies role clarity. Trust-building begins and momentum builds. All of this is a terrific foundation for success.

It may not feel like you're doing much of anything, but a whole lot of magic is happening in the beginning. When project people are given the opportunity to engage in the planning, there is less questioning of the plan later, which slows things down when you need to go fast. When project people participate in the process of thinking through the most expedient path to get up "project mountain," and are encouraged to think differently, they might come up with a creative solution that makes all the difference—like, gee, if speed is the number one priority, then what if we hire a helicopter to take us to the top of the mountain instead? And by the way, is speed really the most important goal? Or is it that we all come back safely (please and thank you very much)?

It's the early planning work that brings the necessary clarity, before project people are knee-deep in the *detail* swamp and complaining. It's when the seeds of trust are planted, so that later they can reach out and grab a team member's shoulder for support when they accidentally misstep.

Take the time you need to identify and line up the best players you can get, make clear who's who, get them pointed in the right direction and starting their journey through Projectland as a team. Together project leadership and the SMEs will move through the teaming process and ultimately work as a unit to deliver the project on time, on budget, on scope, and on quality with a high degree of stakeholder satisfaction.

And who are the stakeholders? Those creatures who may love your project, hate your project, or be finicky fans on the fence somewhere in between those two extremes. Project leaders will need to figure out who they are and what to do about them during planning, otherwise your happy dogs could get underfoot, your finicky flamingos could squawk up a distracting storm, or your sabotaging snakes could jump up and surprise you with a fatal bite.

You now know who's who, how this wild world works, and how important it is to invest the time to get the people part right in the beginning of the project. As the G.I. Joe catchphrase said, "Knowing is half the battle."[2] The other half of the battle is the battle. Get in the game and be the best darn player you can be. I'm cheering you on, screaming my head off, shaking my fist at the referees, and clapping until my hands hurt.

Brave project person, welcome to Projectland.

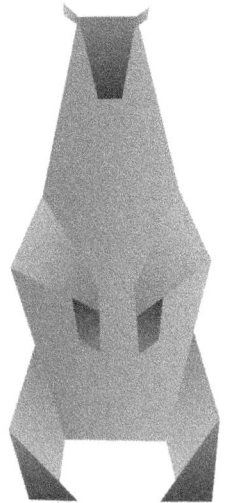

SECTION FOUR
BONUS CONTENT

Because I like to overdeliver a wee bit, and because you made it this far, here's a little bonus content for you.

APPENDIX A
WHERE TO LEARN MORE

A ll the resources associated with this book are available at the Project Guru Press website (projectgurupress.com/meettheplayers/tools).

Check out additional resources listed below for even more learning about how teamwork really can make the dream work in Projectland, including how to access Dawn's micro-learning course, conversations with The Project Gurus, bite-sized tips on social media, and her blog.

THE "SMART TIPS: PROJECT MANAGEMENT & AGILE" MICRO-LEARNING VIDEO COURSE

This is a collection of 39 micro-lessons to help manage projects like a pro, impress your boss and build skills to succeed at work and in life.

Created with and produced by the pros at Udemy, the author's micro-learning video course includes handouts, resources, captions, and a certificate upon completion. As part of Udemy's "Smart Tips" series, videos are 5-minutes'ish or less, covering the project management process in a practical way, more about the Project Management Institute (including certifications), and Agile. As of this writing, approximately 3,000 ambitious learners in nearly 100 countries have joined.

The course's many caption options make it great for global teams who are interested in speaking the same language in Projectland. Captions include but may not be limited to Arabic, Dutch, French, German, Indonesian, Italian, Japanese, Portuguese, Simplified Chinese, Spanish, Turkish, Thai, and Vietnamese. (That's a mouthful in any language!)

Elevate your learning with Smart Tips anytime, anywhere! Udemy's "Smart Tips" is the ultimate micro-learning series. Short, standalone lectures let you learn new skills at your own pace, anytime, anywhere. Find what you need, when you need it. Complete newbies to PMP-certified mentors have given the course 5-star reviews.

HOW TO ACCESS SMART TIPS

If your employer offers Udemy Business, you can access this course right now for free here: https://learning.udemy.com/course/smart-tips-project-management-agile/

If not, don't worry! You can get it using our special referral link here: https://www.udemy.com/course/smart-tips-project-management-agile/?referralCode=022BE9DF78D61A78F7FA

The first few videos are free!

If those links don't cooperate, or you're reading the paper version of this book, go to the Project Guru Press website (projectgurupress.com/meettheplayers/tools) to get the special referral link.

LIVE IN PROJECTLAND: LIVELY LEARNING WITH THE PROJECT GURUS

Check out conversations with your Projectland Tour Guide, Dawn Mahan, and The Project Gurus on topics including, but not limited to:

- Artificial intelligence (AI)
- Certifications
- Change Management
- Design Thinking
- Emotional Intelligence
- Napoleon on Project Leadership

- Project Manager Pain Points
- Product Management

See past episodes here: https://www.projectguruacademy.com/projectland

Subscribe to our page on LinkedIn and plan to join us at our next LIVE event here: https://www.linkedin.com/showcase/projectguruacademy/

Connect with Dawn on Social for bite-sized pro tips and Projectland fun:

- https://www.linkedin.com/in/dawnmahan/
- https://www.instagram.com/dawnjmahan/
- https://twitter.com/pmotiger
- https://www.facebook.com/PMOtiger/
- https://www.youtube.com/@PMOtraining

Visit Dawn's Blog at:
https://www.pmotraining.com/blog

APPENDIX B

QUICK SUMMARY OF ROLES & TOOLS (AKA PROJECTLAND TERMS OF ENDEARMENT)

Italics indicates definitions from the Project Management Institute's Guide to the Project Management Body of Knowledge (PMBOK Guide - Sixth Edition)

Sponsor: *A person or group who provides resources and support for the project, program, or portfolio and is accountable for enabling its success.* Previous editions clarify that "provides resources" often means financial resources, in cash or in kind. When a project is first conceived, the sponsor champions the project. This includes serving as spokesperson to higher levels of management to gather support throughout the organization and promote the benefits that the project will bring. The sponsor leads the project through the engagement or selection process until formally authorized and plays a significant role in the development of the initial scope. For issues that are beyond the control of the project manager, the sponsor serves as an escalation path. The sponsor may also be involved in other important issues such as authorizing changes in scope, phase-end reviews, and go/no-go decisions when risks are particularly high.

Project Manager: *The person assigned by the performing organization to lead the team that is responsible for achieving the project objectives.* This is a challenging, high-profile role with significant responsibility and shifting priorities. It requires flexibility, good judgment, strong leadership, and negotiating skills, and a solid knowledge of project management practices. A project manager must be able to understand project detail but manage from the overall project perspective. The project manager typically occupies the center of the interactions between stakeholders and the project itself.

Team: *A set of individuals who support the project manager in performing the work of the project to achieve its objectives.* A project team is comprised of the project manager, project management team, and other team members who carry out the work but who are not necessarily involved with management of the project. This team is comprised of individuals from different groups with knowledge of a specific subject matter or with a specific skill set who carry out the work of the project.

Team Lead is not a role in the PMBOK Guide but it is a typical role used in practice, particularly for geographically dispersed and larger projects. Team Leads generally report to the project manager and coordinate the work of fellow subject matter experts to plan and create project deliverables.

Thinking Tool: It's not a FORM! Maybe it's a template. Thinking tools provide a framework for THINKING, rather than forms, which folks want to fill out as messily and quickly as possible without much thinking. Remember, no one in the history of the world has ever done this thing before or it wouldn't be called a project. Especially if you think you've done something like this before, this term is a friendly reminder to turn your brains fully to the ON position and think about what is unique about your situation. Most thinking tools are also invitations to engage the right players in the thinking. Two heads are better than one, after all. Pro thinking tools mentioned in this book include the *Stakeholder Analysis & Management Matrix (SAMM)* and corresponding *Communications Plan*, the *High-Level Project Kickoff Thinking Tool*, and your secret weapon to avoid scope creep, the *Work Breakdown Structure (WBS)*.

Stakeholder: *An individual, group or organization that may affect, be affected by, or perceive itself to be affected by a decision, activity, or outcome of a project, program, or portfolio.* WHEW! My translation is that stakeholders are the people outside the team who love your project, hate your project, or are somewhere in between. A stakeholder may also exert influence over the project and its deliverables. It can be helpful to categorize stakeholders as cheerleaders, saboteurs, and finicky fans and create a corresponding plan to manage them throughout the project lifecycle. Use these thinking tools: Stakeholder Analysis & Management Matrix (SAMM) & Communications Plan.

APPENDIX C

THE MEET THE PLAYERS ANIMAL AVATAR CHEAT SHEET

1. **Sponsor** – Lion
2. **Steering Team** – Eagles, Whales, & Owls
3. **Project Manager** – Tiger
4. **Team Leads (Alphas) & Team Members** – Gazelle, Bison, & Dolphin
5. **Stakeholders** – Happy Dog, Flamingo, & Snake

Go to the Project Guru Press website (projectgurupress.com/meettheplayers/tools) to download the infographic, which is way more fun than this boring list.

APPENDIX D
ANIMAL AVATAR ANALYSES

> "I now walk into the wild."
> - Jon Krakauer, Author of "Into the Wild"
> *(based on a true story)*

Humans and animals alike come with traits that can be helpful and perceived as potentially hurtful. The following animal avatar analyses were performed in August 2023 at PMI Minnesota's largest annual event by attendees of a half-day workshop and a one-hour abridged workshop. The descriptions/traits listed were taken verbatim from the flip charts.

As I did not reveal which roles I had selected for each animal before their analysis, these are purely based on the animals themselves. Asterisks (*) indicate upvoting as the half-day workshop participant teams walked around the room, considered each analysis, and offered top marks where they were in highest agreement.

As Socrates suggested, "Know thyself." When you know yourself, and how others might perceive you, you can better aim to be great and contribute positively in Projectland, your organization, family, community, or anywhere you need to interact with other creatures.

This bonus material is intended to help you think about, plan for, and deal with the characteristics of the players you might encounter in your version of Projectland. And, if you are in a particular role, it will help you discover how you may harness the helpful traits for good and avoid potential perceptions of hurtful behaviors. Particularly in the case of steering team members, team members, and stakeholders, where there are several options, you may find yourself gravitating toward one of the creatures. If so, that's the one that you likely have the most in common with or the most to learn from.

PRACTICAL PROJECTLAND CHALLENGE

- Check the animal avatar characteristics related to the role you play in Projectland. Which listed traits resonate most with you? Are there other characteristics that come to mind?
- Which animal avatar most interests you? What do you have in common with it? What can you learn from it?
- What other animal avatars do you believe should be added to the Projectland zoo? Check out the additional ideas offered in Appendix E. If you feel passionate about an animal being added, let me know! Submit your animal avatar idea at the Project Guru Press website (projectgurupress.com/meettheplayers).

Sponsor - Lion

Helpful	Hurtful
• Collaboration (some lions) • Competent • Courageous • Leader • Pack animals/protects the herd • Pioneer/break new ground (not afraid) * • Quick to act/fast decision makers * • Strength • Thin the herd (Shifts resources to the A-team players and leaves them alone to do their thing) • Understand roles • Very vocal/loud - Speaks with authority *	• Alpha male attitude • Attack (unapproachable) • Dominate ** • Don't value detail • Impatient • Intimidating/scary - when the lion roars, all the creatures are on edge, which is distracting them from doing their best work • Lay around a lot (inconsistent) • Maneater • Move too fast/make mistakes • Thin the herd (cruel) • Too stubborn (don't give opportunities to fail)

Steering Team Member - Eagle

Helpful	Hurtful
• Can soar • Cunning * • Excellent hunting/Predator - Focused on the goal/unafraid to remove barriers • Fast on decisions * • Fearless • Foresight * • Good at execution * • Mate for life - committed • Sharp vision ****** • Strong	• Danger to others • Not friendly • Not inclusive • One dimensional • Show off • Solitary/They go it alone • Territorial

Steering Team Member - Whale

Helpful	Hurtful
• Beautiful - attractive + fascinating to watch (Charisma on your steering team can be helpful) • Dive deep ***** • Feed whole town (historically) • Friendly • Hold breath/comes up for air - Balance of "focusing to get stuff done" and "being visible" • Long time with mother - good at developing talent • Powerful ** • Smart • Work in groups *	• Disappears for long time and you don't know where they are • Displaces a lot of water/disruptive • Eats many resources • Eats the little people • Long gestation + long time with mother – takes time to learn, mature, and realize their potential • Size - beached whales hard to return to H2O • Size not as agile • Splash damage • Throws their weight around

Steering Team Member - Owl

Helpful	Hurtful
• 360-degree vision***** • Ability to laser focus ***** • Awake/awareness • Big picture vision • Intelligent • Kills prey • Lean, eliminates waste (e.g., rats) • Listens well • Nocturnal (Good at working the night shift or "burning the midnight oil") • Resilience (wick away troubles e.g., rain, snow/wind) • Top of predator chain • Wise ****	• Doesn't learn from others • Eating your prey turns off/turns away/shuts down collaboration • Flight only • Isolated • Nocturnal (limited hours, too rigid) • Not a team builder • One mode of transit • Too much autonomy (e.g., a negative in an Agile/team centered environment) • Works alone

Project Manager - Tiger

Helpful	Hurtful
• Colorful, stands out • Determined • Fast - speed is key ****** • Focused • Intimidating * • Observers • Protectors • Smart • Strong *******	• Colorful - can become a target • Fast - prove to error ** • Aggressive • Can't climb (limited) • Intimidating * • Predatory • Works alone

Team Member / Subject Matter Expert - Bison

Helpful	Hurtful
• Humble • Methodical • Not afraid/brave (run towards trouble) only animal that runs into the storm *** • Nurturing towards young * • Protective of junior members • Strong * • Team player • Work in groups *	• Bossy (appearance of) * • Conformist • Group think • Look grumpy * • Not agile (appearance of) **** • One track mind • Slow • Soft spoken

Team Member / Subject Matter Expert - Dolphin

Helpful	Hurtful
<ul><li>Agile ****</li><li>Collaborative</li><li>Creative</li><li>Entertainer **</li><li>Fast / agile</li><li>Good communications</li><li>Playful</li><li>Pods/ team matching</li><li>Smart *****</li><li>Teamwork</li><li>Want to help others **</li></ul>	<ul><li>Easily injured *</li><li>Innocent/naive *</li><li>Soft/emotional **</li><li>Too nice (beware of being taken advantage of by evil stakeholders)</li><li>Zero land - not versatile</li></ul>

Team Member / Subject Matter Expert - Gazelle

Helpful	Hurtful
<ul><li>Adaptative****</li><li>Agile</li><li>Alert (excellent at spotting trouble quickly)****</li><li>Confident</li><li>Fast</li><li>Fast decisions</li><li>Listening /hearing **</li><li>Quiet</li><li>Smart</li><li>Work as a team</li></ul>	<ul><li>Group think</li><li>May quit</li><li>Not good listeners</li><li>Scared easily</li><li>Territorial</li><li>Weak</li><li>Won't defend themselves **</li></ul>

Stakeholder: Cheerleader - Happy Dog

Helpful	Hurtful
<ul><li>Can be obedient</li><li>Can be trained and love to work</li><li>Friendly ***</li><li>Have fun</li><li>High energy</li><li>Laugh</li><li>Loyal *****</li><li>Positive attitude</li><li>Protective</li><li>Try new things *</li><li>Welcoming **</li></ul>	<ul><li>Can be nervous/fearful</li><li>Barking and other antics can distract the team</li><li>Friendly/People pleaser (beware of being taken advantage of by evil stakeholders)</li><li>High maintenance</li><li>Lack of focus/Easily distracted (Look! Squirrel!)**</li><li>Lazy (sleep all day)</li><li>Leaves a mess *</li><li>Potentially aggressive, particularly when defending their territory</li><li>Too much enthusiasm * (can get in the way)</li><li>Tough to teach old dogs new tricks</li></ul>

191

Stakeholder: Finicky Fan - Flamingo

Helpful	Hurtful
• Attention getting ****	• Can fly away (can't control)
• Change color (Adaptive) **	• Change color depending on input
• Dancing - energy *	• Dancing (looks good, distracted)
• Effective	• Focused on eating
• Focused (on shrimp)	• Fragile
• Gets a lot done standing on one leg	• Group think (do what everyone else does)
• Looks good doing it	• High visibility all the time
• Part of the group ****	• Lack solo skills
• Rise above the muck	• Not always clear why doing what they're doing
• Works well in group	• Of questionable value

Stakeholder: Saboteur - Snake

Helpful	Hurtful
• Adaptable	• Bite hurts others ***** (negative perception)
• Bite hurts others (self-defense)	• Can constrict/injure
• Colorful - some are neon	• Creepy
• Can creep - enables focused work	• Dangerous
• Cunning *	• Frightening
• Kills pests (vermin)	• Hides easily
• Size - fits everywhere ***	• Poisons (some snakes)
• Stealthy *	• Trampled underfoot
• Thermal sensitivity	
• Very mobile	

APPENDIX E
ADDITIONAL ANIMAL AVATARS
IN THE PROJECTLAND ZOO

Workshop participants offered additional animal avatar suggestions and analyses, plus my editor and I threw in a few extras because we couldn't help ourselves!

Bear

- Helpful: Adaptive, omnivore, protective
- Hurtful: Intimidating, hibernates – not productive all year round

Elephant

- Helpful: memory, powerful, strong, intelligent
- Hurtful: Intimidating, temper, too overbearing

Hawaiian Hoary Bat – Hawaii has no native land mammals aside from the tiny Hawaiian Hoary Bat

- Helpful: Eats bugs; Unique, just like projects
- Hurtful: A reclusive and rarely seen creature. This reminds us of the folks who are never in the office and hard to pin down. The worst of these is the sponsor who assigns a

project, says "let me know when it's done," does nothing to help guide it along the way, and then is disappointed at the end when they are somehow surprised that it does not meet their expectations that they didn't explain well in the beginning.

Horse

- Helpful: Agile, trainable/learner, protective, resilient, strong, some breeds are "workhorses"
- Hurtful: High maintenance, expensive, minds of their own, can be skittish and buck off the rider, run away when they sense danger

Donkey

- Helpful: Stand their ground when they sense trouble, great companions, form strong bonds with trusted people and animals, strong for their size, smart
- Hurtful: Take time to trust, noisy when they want something, can be stubborn, get bored easily, not adaptive to inclement weather, stoic (hard to tell when they're hurting), can become saboteurs if ignored

Duck, Goose, Swan, and other Waterfowl

- Helpful: Unique ability to get down into the weeds, fly above the forest and see the big picture, and also calmly glide across the water while paddling like crazy under the surface.
- Hurtful: Too much quacking or honking can annoy folks and cause them to tune out or worse.

Monkey

- Helpful: Agile, curious, fun, knows the customer, many skills, team player
- Hurtful: Can be spiteful and cause chaos

Rabbit

- Helpful: Agile, keen awareness, social and affectionate, their feet are considered lucky (we'll take all the help we can get in Projectland!)
- Hurtful: Rapidly multiply, wreak havoc on the garden, skittish; can be bratty, willful, and even destructive

Spider

- Helpful: "Bug" killers, have six to eight eyes (good visibility), execution, no oversight required, multi-tasking
- Hurtful: Can tangle unsuspecting creatures in a web of drama

Unicorn

- Helpful: Aspirational goals can be motivating and useful (e.g., zero safety incidents), intelligent, calming, and can fix things with magic
- Hurtful: Too good to be true

Sloth

- Helpful: Easy to track them down because they don't travel far, they appear to smile even when they're experiencing pain or stress, they bring a different perspective (90% of life spent hanging upside down), can serve as the lookout (can turn head and obtain almost 360-degree view of surroundings)
- Hurtful: Takes forever to get the simplest thing done, and no amount of prodding will change this.

Prairie Dogs and Meerkats

- Helpful: Agile, great team players (work together to create colonies), good at building things and finding a way to adapt, excellent communicators, critically necessary for the ecosystem
- Hurtful: Can go unnoticed until they climb out of their hole and speak up; can be territorial to protect their team

Seagull

- Helpful: Cleans up messes, has a global outlook (the only seabird that spans all seven continents)
- Hurtful: Swoops down, makes a lot of noise, makes a mess, and flies off

Starfish

- Helpful: Resilient. If you cut off an arm, they grow a new one. Tough skin.
- Hurtful: Hard to find initially, slow moving, they're brainless

Zebra

- Helpful: Brings beauty to the landscape, social, strong communication skills
- Hurtful: Causes confusion; there is only black and white with them, no gray

ACKNOWLEDGMENTS

EXTRA SPECIAL HUMANS

Without my brilliant author and project guru friend Jerry Manas, this book would never have seen the light. Your unwavering, unconditional, and chapter-by-chapter accountability partner support, smart suggestions, and pro edits have transformed this book into something I can be proud to share. He also found our talented cover artist, Kerry Ellis, and they both endured what must have felt like an endless set of iterations to arrive at the wild cover featuring origami animals that you see today. Sorry and thank you both for your patience with my newbieness!

To Laura Barnard, 2021 Global PMO influencer of the Year, for sending me AJ Harper's book, *Write a Must-Read*, with a handwritten note of encouragement. AJ's advice and especially the SFD concept made a huge difference in my being able to overcome my fears and perfectionist tendencies.

To Crystal Richards for introducing me to the pros at Udemy, who not only didn't laugh at my animal avatar concept, but also said they loved them and then proceeded to hire me to be their expert to develop the course of mini-lessons I had years earlier envisioned. Without your vote of confidence, my animals would have gone the way of the dodo bird.

To all of the colleagues and clients who I've had the privilege of working with in Projectland, thank you! Extra special thanks to "Butterfly Beth" Montgomery for her creativity, encouragement, and launch support, as well as to Ricardo Brett for transcribing the PMI Minnesota animal analyses flipcharts to softcopy.

BOOK INSIDER VIPS

Many thanks to everyone who signed up, showed up on Zoom, and provided helpful feedback. You gave me the courage to continue, inspired me to make progress, and made the process of writing much more fun and less lonely. When my work stalled, and strategy pivoted, you nudged me and reminded me to harness that big cat courage required to keep going. Sincere thanks! Because gamification is fun and motivating for some, Book Insider VIPs are listed in order of participation points.

Jerry Manas, Jesse Middaugh, John Salah, Corey Scheick, Dave Lozinger, Andy Vance, Mollie Coats, Ricardo Brett, Vashti Brown, Peter Canino, Matt Carpenter, Rosalind Guy, Juan Ramirez, Beth Montgomery, Nohma Abboud, Ralph Ruocco, Sheila Black, Vasu Marti, Michael Schafer, Curtis Jenkins, Samuel Barnes, Gregory Wilson, Nicole Hodge, Iris Florea, Dorothy Coleman, Michael D. Hilbert, David Hale Sylvester, Roman Voloshenko, Debra Hanzlik, Dr. Laura Dowling, Michael Carr, Christopher Boop, Monique Johnson, Paul Hundertmark, Sean Malak, Yana Hewlett, Suresh Chelliah, Michelle Garrison, Sandeep Dhareshwar, Kathryn Kinsey, James W. Smith, Tom Emmerth, Christine Donnelly, Alicia Malley, Pamela McChalicher, Ian McKenzie, Cathy Fisher, Ina Tubilleja, Dave Broderick, Yusak Rabin, Robert Musilli, Tina Underhill, Luiza Sanz

PROJECT MANAGEMENT INSTITUTE (PMI) MINNESOTA CHAPTER

Many thanks to PMI Minnesota for inviting me to speak and allowing me to bring the whole Projectland Zoo! Extra special thanks to Michael Schafer who was the very best sherpa! While many preferred to remain anonymous, PMI Minnesota participants who gave their permission to thank them here are: Betsy Khan, Brian Klinga, David Owen, Jeff Serba, John Lewis, Maria Acosta, and Michelle McManus.

EARLY READERS & FEEDBACK GIVERS

Thank you for your enthusiastic, honest feedback, and input to make the book stronger!

Aline Oliveira, Bevin Ann Buchheister, Esq., Caroline Gudel, Janna Horn, Jerry Manas, Jesse Middaugh, Kate Wegener, Michael Allen Welch, Jr., Rosalind Guy, Steph Honami

Thank you to the many PMI Vietnam "Storytelling for Project People" Workshop hosts and participants, especially the following ambitious professionals who provided their enthusiastic support of the book: An Le, Hai Van Nguyen, Hieu Nguyen, Huy-Cuong Duong, John Phan Duong, Thao Nguyen, Tinh Nguyen, Tran Mai Anh, Vu Trung Kien, and Vu Bien.

Heartfelt thanks to the following supporters of my work who generously spent countless hours to provide instrumental feedback:

Anne Wilms, Former Fortune 500 Chief Information Officer (CIO)

Cathy Fisher, Founder & President, Quistem, LLC; Global Expert in the Automotive Industry

Grace Duffy, President, Management and Performance Systems; Author; American Society for Quality (ASQ) Fellow; 2014 Quality Magazine Person of the Year; 2016 International Woman of Quality

Jim Rommens, Graduate Adjunct Instructor in Project Management, Co-Author of *The Expert Test Manager: Guide to the ISTQB Expert Level Certification*

Malcolm Hobson, Former Global Project Director

Katrina Featherston, Kentucky State Police Forensic Laboratory Quality Assurance Supervisor

Michael Kovach, Former Chief Technology Officer; Principal, FutureWAN

Michael Stubblefield, CEO, Avantor; Former Senior Expert, McKinsey & Company

Rick Gaynor, Former CFO for many public and private equity owned global companies

Dr. Roger Korman, Former CEO, DMD Digital Health Connections Group

Dr. Stuart M. Smith, President, Targeted Performance Solutions; University Professor

ABOUT THE AUTHOR

Dawn Mahan is the founder of PMOtraining, LLC. She is a dynamic international speaker, a Project Management Institute (PMI) certified leader with extensive global experience, and sole inventor of the *ProjectFlo® Process Learning System* that makes learning PMI's complex process fast, easy, and fun. She works with C-level leaders, business owners in growth mode, PMO leaders, and project managers at all levels. Her work in preparing young professionals in the YearUp program for internships at major companies has been featured in Morningstar, Yahoo! Finance and more.

Dawn started her writing career in high school when she became a published poet and won the English award at graduation. Then, the practicalities of life took over and she found herself pursuing degrees and work in STEM fields. In the early 2000s she finally got back to writing when she collaborated with colleagues on a blog they named *PMthink! Project Management Thought Leadership*, and, as she was the only female in the troupe, she assumed the Austin Powers-esque moniker, FemPM.

In 2009, she left the Fortune 50 and started her own firm. In 2014, she was awarded Professional of the Year Consulting/Project Management by Strathmore Who's Who Worldwide. In 2021, she was hired by Udemy as their project management expert to co-create *Smart Tips: Project Management & Agile* for their business and marketplace platforms. She has trained thousands of ambitious professionals around the world.

Dawn has built houses in Cambodia with Habitat for Humanity, has played a variety of roles on the American Lung Association's Philadelphia Leadership Board, and sponsors a girls flag football team in Florida.

When she's not in Projectland, you can most often find her with family in Hawaii, Pennsylvania, or the Florida Keys.

SPECIAL NOTE FROM DAWN MAHAN

Thank you so much for reading *Meet the Players in Projectland*! If you've enjoyed this book, please consider taking a few moments to post a short review on the retailer of your choice. I would greatly appreciate it, and your honest review may help other project people discover the book.

Please consider this your personal VIP invitation to join me and our project gurus in Projectland on your favorite social platform and/or at an upcoming event in the virtual or real world.

The best way to join us and be notified of upcoming learning opportunities (many of which are free) is to join our mailing list on PMOtraining.com (https://www.pmotraining.com/contact-us).

Wishing you all the best in Projectland and beyond!

Sincerely,
Dawn

NOTES

INTRODUCTION: A NOT SO FUN FACT & WHY YOU NEED THIS BOOK

1. https://www.peanuts.com/about/pigpen
2. "The Most Important Business Book of the Year: 'How Big Things Get Done'," January 4, 2024, Source: https://www.inc.com/video/the-most-important-business-book-of-the-year-how-big-things-get-done.html
3. Black, K. (1996). Causes of project failure: a survey of professional engineers. PM Network, 10(11), 21–24. Source: https://www.pmi.org/learning/library/causes-project-failure-survey-engineers-4814
4. "The 6 not-so-obvious reasons a project plan fails," February 8, 2019, Source: https://www.microsoft.com/en-us/microsoft-365/business-insights-ideas/resources/the-6-not-so-obvious-reasons-a-project-plan-fails
5. Learn more about this incredible non-profit here: https://www.yearup.org/about

1. WHAT IS A PROJECT? WHAT IS NOT?

1. https://www.goodreads.com/quotes/tag/clarity
2. Project Management Institute, *A Guide to the Project Management Body of Knowledge (PMBOK Guide®)* - Sixth Edition, page 715 (Newtown Square, PA: Project Management Institute, 2017)

2. WELCOME TO PROJECTLAND

1. Abraham Maslow Quotes. BrainyQuote.com, BrainyMedia Inc, 2023. https://www.brainyquote.com/quotes/abraham_maslow_752792, accessed December 22, 2023.
2. Alfred P. Sloan Quotes. BrainyQuote.com, BrainyMedia Inc, 2023. https://www.brainyquote.com/quotes/alfred_p_sloan_194036, accessed December 22, 2023.

3. IS PROJECT MANAGEMENT JUST LIKE MANAGEMENT?

1. https://pennbookcenter.com/leadership-vs-management-quotes/
2. https://www.cbsnews.com/news/are-you-a-leader-or-a-manager-marcus-buckingham-says-you-cant-be-both/ accessed on February 19, 2024. Marcus Buckingham, author of *First, Break all the Rules*, is one of the instrumental founders of the strengths revolution. Source: https://www.tmbc.com/our-story/
3. https://www.apm.org.uk/resources/what-is-project-management/ accessed February 19, 2024. Definition from APM Body of Knowledge 7th edition.

4. WHO'S WHO IN PROJECTLAND

1. Project Management Institute, *A Guide to the Project Management Body of Knowledge (PMBOK Guide)* - Sixth Edition, page 723 (Newtown Square, PA: Project Management Institute, 2017).

5. I'M THE SPONSOR, HEAR ME ROAR

1. https://www.britannica.com/topic/Buridans-ass

7. THE PROJECT MANAGER: NOT QUITE THE KING (OR QUEEN!) OF THE JUNGLE, BUT AWFULLY CLOSE

1. Hat tip to Dr. Seuss.
2. Source: Building the High-Performance Project Management Function, PMO Executive Council 2007
3. Hat tip to our Design Thinking Project Guru, J.K. Chua, for suggesting this addition.

8. THE DREAM TEAM: THE FAST, THE STRONG, & THE FURIOUSLY FUN

1. https://your.yale.edu/learn-and-grow-how-teamwork-makes-dream-work
2. USA's 1992 Olympics Dream Team: Basketball super galacticos. Article updated on 08 September 2022. https://olympics.com/en/news/usa-1992-olympics-dream-team-basketball-super-galacticos
3. Federation Rule Change Opens Olympics to N.B.A. Players. New York Times, April 8, 1989. https://www.nytimes.com/1989/04/08/sports/federation-rule-change-opens-olympics-to-nba-players.html
4. https://european-union.europa.eu/institutions-law-budget/euro/history-and-purpose_en
5. https://www.epa.gov/laws-regulations/summary-clean-air-act
6. https://www.epa.gov/history/epa-history-clean-air-act-amendments-1990
7. https://www.epa.gov/archive/epa/aboutepa/epa-regulates-dry-cleaners-first-air-toxics-rule-under-new-clean-air-act.html
8. Huffington, Arianna, *Thrive: The Third Metric to Redefining Success and Creating a Life of Well-Being, Wisdom, and Wonder* (New York, NY: Harmony, 2014)
9. Many thanks to Jeff Serba, who ran up to me after my talk to excitedly share that the bison go toward the storm, which I didn't know. The official source: National Bison Association: The Nature of Bison - https://bisoncentral.com/the-bison-advantage/
10. Source: U.S. Department of the Interior: https://www.doi.gov/blog/15-facts-about-our-national-mammal-american-bison; Accessed February 25, 2024
11. "Top 10 Facts About Dolphins," WWF-UK, https://www.wwf.org.uk/learn/fascinating-facts/dolphins
12. The phrase "Plan your work and work your plan," among other variations, has been attributed to multiple parties, including Napoleon Hill, Margaret Thatcher, Vince Lombardi, and others.

13. When tasks on the critical path are late, the project end date is impacted too. Other tasks that can be done in parallel to the critical path do not impact the project end date.
14. Duckworth, Angela, *Grit: The Power of Passion and Perseverance* (New York, NY: Scribner, 2018) - I listened to the author narrate the audiobook and absolutely loved it.
15. https://www.reaganfoundation.org/ronald-reagan/nancy-reagan/her-causes/

9. THREE SURPRISING KINDS OF STAKEHOLDERS

1. https://www.goodreads.com/quotes/699462-you-can-please-some-of-the-people-all-of-the

10. LOVE THE CREATURES YOU'RE WITH

1. Since two United States presidents quoted *Jerry Maguire*, I figured I could too. This now famous scene made Gooding an instant success and propelled the actor to a best supporting actor Oscar win. https://www.usatoday.com/story/life/movies/2016/12/12/jerry-maguire-anniversary-tom-cruise-show-me-money/95300458/
2. Damien is a name that's Greek in origin and means to tame or subdue. The name Damien still can run a chill down the spine of people who were raised in the 1970s. It's the name of the main character in *The Omen* film franchise, a child who is the Antichrist. The franchise was so popular, it led to a remake in 2006. Source: https://momlovesbest.com/evil-and-demon-baby-names
3. Thanks to Indonesia-based Project Guru Jonathan Kine for this simple explanation.

12. GET READY FOR THE STORM: TEAMING IS A PROCESS, TOO

1. "I Can't Accept Not Trying: Michael Jordan on the Pursuit of Excellence," (1994) by Michael Jordan, Mark Vancil and Sandro Miller Source: https://www.entrepreneur.com/living/12-motivational-quotes-from-michael-jordan/325840
2. The TV series "Cheers" (1982-1993) won 28 Primetime Emmys. Actor George Wendt played the character Norm Peterson in 270 episodes. Source: https://www.imdb.com/title/tt0083399/
3. https://your.yale.edu/learn-and-grow-how-teamwork-makes-dream-work

13. YOUR SECRET WEAPON TO GET THE PLAYERS ROWING IN THE SAME DIRECTION

1. Source: https://www.espn.com/classic/quotes_Lombardi.html
2. https://www.profootballhof.com/players/vince-lombardi/

14. YOUR SECRET WEAPON PART TWO: WHEN PART ONE JUST ISN'T ENOUGH

1. Pardon the Austin Powers reference, I just couldn't help myself!

15. YOU'RE OFF TO THE RACES!

1. Mario Andretti's racing career spanned over five decades and he remains an ambassador today. A champion in Formula One, Champ Car, dirt tracks, and a winner at the Indy 500, Daytona 500, and 12 Hours of Sebring, few drivers can match Andretti's success. In 2000, he was named Driver of the Century by Racer magazine. Source: https://www.automotivehalloffame.org/honoree/mario-andretti/

2. G.I. Joe was an action figure who, to placate parents, ended each of his 1980s cartoons with the PSA, "Now you know. And knowing is half the battle…" The PSA was given within the context of something dangerous kids did unintentionally – like running out into traffic. Source: https://psyne.co/the-g-i-joe-fallacy-knowing-is-half-the-battle-right/

www.ingramcontent.com/pod-product-compliance
Lightning Source LLC
Chambersburg PA
CBHW052111030426
42335CB00025B/2931